Uma Girish is a certified speaker and bereavement vol about helping women find m ...aken to new purpose. Her writing has ... in seven countries and several of her short stories ...ve won awards. Uma writes a grief blog called 'The Grammar of the Grief' and hosts a weekly eponymous Internet radio show for the Creating Calm Network on Blog Talk Radio. She also facilitates a grief group at a retirement community. You can contact Uma at www.umagirish.com

———<◦◦◦◦◦◦◦◦>———

With exquisite detail and total compassion, Uma sculpts the heartbreak of losing her parents and finding the beauty of the spiritual blessing that comes from a broken heart. She allows the reader to feel her pain and walk with her as she breaks through to the glorious side of God's love. Sharing the differences of the Hindu culture with the American way of death, Uma gives us a clear picture of the universal potential of grief: moving forward to serve all mankind with unconditional love. Thank you, Uma, for sharing your courage and wisdom.

– Lo Anne Mayer,
author of *Celestial Conversations:Healing Relationships After Death*

To Sudhir,
with love & gratitude,
Uma
6/3/2014

LOSING
Amma,
FINDING HOME

A memoir about love, loss and life's detours

Uma Girish

HAY HOUSE INDIA
Australia • Canada • Hong Kong • India
South Africa • United Kingdom • United States

Hay House Publishers (India) Pvt. Ltd.
Muskaan Complex, Plot No.3, B-2 Vasant Kunj, New Delhi-110 070, India
Hay House Inc., PO Box 5100, Carlsbad, CA 92018-5100, USA
Hay House UK, Ltd., Astley House, 33 Notting Hill Gate, London W11 3JQ, UK
Hay House Australia Pty Ltd., 18/36 Ralph St., Alexandria NSW 2015, Australia
Hay House SA (Pty) Ltd., PO Box 990, Witkoppen 2068, South Africa
Hay House Publishing, Ltd., 17/F, One Hysan Ave., Causeway Bay, Hong Kong
Raincoast, 9050 Shaughnessy St., Vancouver, BC V6P 6E5, Canada
Email: contact@hayhouse.co.in
www.hayhouse.co.in

Author's photo courtesy: Tiffany Joe Bibby

ISBN 978-93-81398-80-7

Printed and bound at
Rajkamal Electric Press, Sonepat, Haryana (India)

To Amma and Appa ... my wings and my roots ...

thank you for letting me

soar in uncharted skies

Acknowledgements

A heartfelt thank you to my writing buddies who helped shape and craft this book with critiques, coffee and comfort: Sheri, Chris, Rita, Emily, Sandi and Sharon.

I would also like to thank Sanjana, Tulika, Ravi and the entire Hay House team for making my dream come true in the best possible way.

Thank you, Girish for always holding my hand, and Ruki for sharing my love of writing.

PROLOGUE

27 January 2009

As I WALK OUT FRESH FROM A SHOWER FOLLOWING A sweaty session with a Jane Fonda DVD, I don't have the faintest inkling that eight thousand five hundred miles away, on the other side of the world, my mother is breathing her last.

It is a raw January morning in a Chicago suburb. My fourteen-year-old daughter, Ruki, a high school sophomore, is away at school. My husband, Girish, is in Indianapolis on a business trip, and expected home in a few hours.

My brother, Mahesh, called last night, expressed a dilemma familiar to immigrants with an ailing parent overseas. Should he book his ticket, get on a plane to Chennai, so our youngest sister, Maya, who is holding the fort will feel supported? Or should he wait a couple more days? Something nagged at him, he said, a strange, unnamable feeling urging him to go. And yet, there are practical considerations. He has a wife who doesn't drive, a toddler, and a twenty-two-hour journey across the oceans. Like any responsible husband/father/employee, he needs to consolidate: balance affairs at home and the workplace and apply for a leave of absence before he books his ticket.

'Sleep on it. Sometimes, things look clearer by the cold light of day,' I'd offered, unsure myself.

Now, my landline is ringing. I grab it, fully expecting to hear his voice.

'Mahesh,' I say.

Nothing else about that call is expected – not my brother's tone, nor his words, or the meaning they convey. Nothing. It is the wrong phone call on the wrong day at the wrong time.

'Uma,' he starts gingerly. After a long pause, he speaks the words that break me; tear me limb from limb; splinter my soul. 'Amma's ... left us.'

'What?'

It is a combination of stunned disbelief and certain knowing coalescing into that single-syllable word. It is all I can muster during such a momentous occasion, as my world tilts on its axis. It will be a long time before it rights itself, if ever.

I hear him, his words rushing past my bewildered brain, like the landscape outside a train window. 'Brace yourself ... calm down ... take it easy.'

I had spoken to Amma just three days ago. The tired drawl in her voice was a red flag of sorts, but when I mentioned it to Maya (whom my parents lived with), she'd attributed it to the meds; said they made Amma woozy. I bought into it readily, shrugged off the concern, comfortably slid to the corner called 'denial', preferring to hide there, far away from the light.

My cell phone rings; it is my brother-in-law from Chennai.

I can barely remember how the phone conversation with Mahesh ends.

I feel heavy, weighed down by raw emotion. As my brother-in-law starts to speak, I say to him, 'Yeah, I know. Mahesh just called me,' flinching from yet another repetition.

'How did this happen?' I wonder aloud, knowing he cannot possibly have the cosmic consolation I seek. I ask to talk to Maya who is falling apart in a friend's arms at Santhosh Hospital where Amma's cold, lifeless body lies.

Thousands of miles away from each other, connected by a fragile transatlantic connection, we cry together.

I hang up and sink down to the carpeted floor of the living room numbed, shaken, terrified. When I manage to pick myself up, I rush to the altar and rage at God. 'How can I go on without her?' I ask a mute Higher Power. I'd never imagined a world without her. Who do I call when I need a home remedy for a tummy ache? Or a recipe when friends are coming for dinner? I switch on my laptop. Her gentle smiling face is my screensaver. I weep like a child.

Through the fog clouding my brain, I know I have to call Girish. I try his cell phone thrice. Each time I hear his voicemail say he can't take my call. What kind of a message do you leave in these circumstances? *Hi, I'm calling to say Amma passed away at half-past nine in the night India time. Please call me back when you have a moment.*

Outside the window, piles of snow border the curb. A white blanket smothers the life of the grassy slope, shrouds the picnic table and benches. Stark-limbed trees stand bereft, mirroring my mood. All alone in my apartment, I alternate between heaving sobs and a strange, frightening calm when I can't feel my own heartbeat.

My mind rewinds to that beautiful, bright summer day only eight months ago – 25 May 2008 – when the e-mail arrived. It came from Maya, hurling through cyberspace at the gentle click of a mouse button, dropped into my inbox without as much as a whisper. But the power it had, to turn my new life one hundred and eighty degrees is not something I'm likely to forget for a long, long time.

ONE

May – December 2008

1

May 2008

I'VE NOW COME TO UNDERSTAND THIS: WHAT STARTS OUT as a perfect blue-sky cumulus-cloud day rarely ends as one. It strikes me how I meandered through days and weeks in a haze, unappreciative of the magic in simple moments.

That truth came home to me on 25 May, exactly thirty-two days after I set foot on American soil as a green card holder. The warm, buttery sunshine of that morning masked an imminent thunderstorm. Soon, lightning would slash my soft-blue sky into shreds.

As Girish Google-mapped our destination and drove the twenty-six miles to Chicago Botanic Garden, I was blissfully deluded. Intoxicated by gardens glistening in the spring sunshine, my faith in the continued existence of this picture-perfect setting was absolute.

When we returned home, pleasantly tired after the fun trip, I opened my laptop. Quickly, I punched in my password and wrote a chatty e-mail to Maya about our latest sightseeing trip and new discoveries. Then, I clicked the incoming mail icon; sure that Maya's overnight e-mail was waiting for me. It was; just not the one I was expecting.

The words exploded at me like little rocks. 'Amma's right breast … hard as a rock … swollen nipple … mammogram at the hospital … scheduling ultrasound and biopsy …'

Each phrase smacked me hard in the middle of my chest, the soft space where all my love for Amma resided. The euphoria of

15

the morning vanished. It was like peeling the corner of a Magna Doodle and watching the words you wrote on it a moment ago vanish.

Unbidden, a visual slid into my mind's eye: A teary-eyed Amma in a nightie with blue flowers printed on it, holding a bon voyage card. We'd gone to say our goodbyes en route to the international airport. Was that only a month ago? And I'd had no idea of the invisible monster that lurked between us, inside her, giggling, rubbing its hands in glee, and waiting for the opportune moment to topple our worlds.

I must have read Maya's e-mail hundreds of times: the words swirling, colliding, twisting out of shape and form, unintelligible things on a computer screen. A fraction of a second later, it struck me. I'd gushed about the architectural marvels in downtown Chicago and the wonders of Field Museum of Natural History; she'd been in a doctor's office listening to the somber tones creep into an oncologist's voice as he declared doom and gloom on our family. Guilt slugged me in the gut.

When the fog of emotion lifted some, I began to absorb the truth. Amma had noticed redness and swelling in her breasts as early as February – four months ago – but had ignored it until now.

Maya's e-mail confirmed that Amma's medical reports were due four days from today. May be, just may be, there was a sliver of a chance that it wasn't as bad as it looked. I pleaded and bargained with God; convinced myself I was going to wake up from a nightmare any minute now. I raged at Him; apologized, before pleading and bargaining again.

2

*W*HEN I EVENTUALLY SWITCHED ON MY LAPTOP AND CHECKED my inbox, all the hope that had buoyed my chest like a helium balloon whooshed out. The confirmation on Maya's e-mail devastated me.

Amma has cancer.

Even though her earlier e-mail indicated that this was a distinct possibility the news rocked me. Those words took over the rest of my day. Those three terrible words were everywhere I looked: On the oatmeal-coloured carpet, the living room walls, the green grassy slopes outside the window. I could've handled 'Amma fell in the bathroom', or 'Amma has a bout of viral flu', or 'Amma had a bad asthma attack'. But CANCER! I couldn't even see that word belong in the same sentence as Amma.

Then the cold, hard facts hit me. The cancer was big; it had spread to most of her right breast; the next steps were to stall the enemy, keep it from invading her lungs and liver. The ultrasound and mammogram presented damaging evidence. The doctors were already talking about a chemo schedule, possibly breast surgery.

Girish and I broke the news to Ruki, who instinctively reverted to being my child, crawled into my lap and sobbed her heart out. The three of us stood in front of the tiny altar we'd fashioned, lit the lamp, held hands and whispered a fervent prayer. It was one of those moments when I didn't even know what to pray for. Do I pray for the doctors to discover they'd made a terrible mistake? That the cancer not be as bad as everyone thought it was? Or, that Amma go through surgery and come out clean on the other side?

We'd arrived in this country exactly forty days ago, flying into Indianapolis where Girish's sister and family gave us a start. We stayed with them for three weeks, becoming 'legitimate'. By mid-May we had our Social Security cards and credit cards, a rented apartment in Schaumburg, and a second-hand Toyota Corolla: enough to make a new beginning.

When you're literally one month old in a new country and ten days old in a new city, life doesn't stop – even if your mother is battling cancer. You don't have the luxury of putting time on hold. We still had to eat. Ruki still had to start her sophomore year in school. School enrollment forms had to be filled out. So that's what I did, I spent an entire afternoon writing out the mundane details of our life: address, phone numbers, occupation, emergency contact person, etc.

In the afternoon, Girish and I drove to IKEA to shop for new mattresses. After struggling to respond to a bunch of inane questions – 'Do you sleep on your back or stomach?' 'Do you feel hot or cold at night?' 'Do you like a soft mattress or a firm one?' 'Latex or spring?' – we arrived home with three memory-foam mattresses. Loading them into the IKEA van, unloading them in our apartment parking lot and lugging them up the stairs was a reprieve, however brief, from the personal nightmare I found myself trapped in.

When I crawled into bed that night, I hardly felt the joy of the new mattress that moulded to the contours of my body, as IKEA had promised. A corny poster slogan – 'Money can buy you a mattress; it can't buy you sleep' – slid into my mind and kept me awake for a long time.

I wondered if Amma was sleeping tonight.

3

At the first stirrings of consciousness my mind clenched, attempting to shut out all thoughts. Much as I wanted to remain in that space of blankness, it was only three seconds before my mind screamed the words. AMMA HAS CANCER!

Soon, it was like a frantic CNN news-crawl inside my head, every thought reflecting fear, anger and guilt.

God has a weird sense of humour. Why were we brought to a new country and a new life, when Amma was going to be diagnosed with a potentially life-threatening illness just five weeks later? Had Amma suspected it? Had she kept it a secret because she saw us packing our bags, getting ready to embark on an overseas adventure? Would we have changed our plans had we known in February?

Girish's successor in Chennai had already been appointed; Girish's paperwork to move to his new position in Chicago was already in the works. Knowing about Amma's cancer at the time would definitely have made the move heart-wrenching. There would have been a truckload of guilt to carry.

My mind was spinning at furious speed, struggling to analyze the situation, break it into bite-sized pieces that I could swallow.

My second sister, Vidu, lived in Bahrain with her husband and their four-year-old son, Abu. *Did she know about Amma's diagnosis? Had Maya called her?*

Throughout the motions of cooking, cleaning, washing and eating, the horrible truth nagged at me, an itch I was unable to ignore: Amma has cancer and is walking around clueless about the seriousness of the diagnosis. Maya's e-mail also said they were getting a second opinion, and would only tell Amma if the diagnosis matched the first. A second opinion wouldn't change much, not at this stage. My heart went out to my little sister, six years younger to me, who suddenly found herself in the middle of this awful predicament. I was now eight thousand five hundred miles away from her whereas, even a month ago, I'd lived only five minutes away.

My husband and daughter were right beside me, and yet I felt alone. I yearned to connect with a sibling, someone who shared a flesh-and-blood bond with me as Amma's child. Maya and I were in different time zones, but I did have a sibling in my backyard: My brother, Mahesh, who had for the last seven or eight years snapped ties with everyone in the family – except for my parents. The only piece of information my sisters and I had was that he lived in Chicago. We didn't have a street address or a telephone number, just an old e-mail address. Maya had only e-mailed him the basic diagnosis, nothing more. He'd e-mailed us all in shock and provided a cell phone number. My husband suggested I call him. It took me about two seconds to make that decision. I could save him some anxious moments before Maya's next update arrived in his inbox.

I picked up the phone and dialled his number.

⋖⋗

It's difficult to know what to say to a person you've spent the last decade of your life trying to hate – especially when he's on the other end of a phone line.

The how and why of our dispute had become submerged in all the ugly emotional turbulence that had churned over the years. My parents, sisters, and I were aligned on one side; Mahesh and his wife on the other. As things unravelled even more, extended family members had become entangled, taken sides. As most conflicts go, the threads were lost over the years; however, the emotions surrounding the protagonists continued to remain charged.

My brother and his wife had chosen to alienate themselves, restricting contact to my parents alone; not difficult to do given that his work took him on a series of postings all over the world. For the record, it must be stated that he never once forgot his filial duty, conscientiously mailing a generous cheque home every month. My parents' domestic expenses had grown steep since Appa's brain injury fifteen years ago – he now needed 24/7 nursing care.

In the interim, an attempt at peace was made while Mahesh was posted for a brief time in Chennai. As tradition dictates – the son and his wife shoulder the responsibility of caring for the parents – Amma and Appa moved in with them in 2004, four years after his marriage. What happened during those brief months will remain a mystery to us. Amma's version was completely at odds with Mahesh's version. In less than six months Amma approached Maya, who was single at the time and sharing an apartment with a friend. She asked if Maya would consider a situation where the three of them could live together.

Amma, Appa and Maya moved into a shoebox of an apartment a couple of months later. The apartment they now lived in was much nicer. They had been living under the same roof for four and a half years now.

⋖⋗⋖⋗

Here Mahesh was, on the line and I needed to be civil. I stuck to the business on hand: Amma's diagnosis.

'It's confirmed. Stage 4 …' I couldn't bring myself to utter the ugly word.

'It seemed serious ... even without the second opinion,' he said.

'How is it possible ... I mean, I saw her barely a month ago. She seemed fine. Doing all the usual stuff ... cooking, watching her soaps, fixing Appa's TV.'

'These things just show up, I guess. Not everyone gets a warning.'

A few moments into the conversation, the realization startled me. The bad blood between us had somehow ebbed away, leaving room for the connection we so badly needed at this moment. All that mattered right now was we shared the same blood – the same Amma, the same Appa.

He told me he lived about eighteen miles away, from Schaumburg, in Naperville. Even if physical proximity was all we could have for now, it was enough.

I thought back to that single moment, one that causes the hair on the back of my neck to stand up even today. As soon as Girish's company had confirmed his new station of work – Chicago – I'd asked Amma which part of the US Mahesh lived in: Her whispered reply – 'Chicago' – had taken my breath away. This had to be more than a coincidence. A bigger force was at work here.

Mahesh called again the next day. We ended up having a nice, easy conversation this time. It was familiar and comforting, this voice from my past, one I'd stopped hearing for years. A voice that had, for so long grated with recriminations and allegations now softened with reassuring cadences.

⋘ ⋙

My days had their ups and downs. There were brief moments – while I sipped a creamy latte or was distracted by the architecture of a house at the corner of a winding lane – when I snapped ties with my depressing reality. After all, I was still adjusting to life in a new country, a new culture. Soon, truth, lurking behind a thin veil, would step out and gnaw at the pleasant illusion of normalcy I'd begun to create.

Today I was mad at God. Some families never get a break from cosmic avalanches, it appears, and we happen to be one of them: Addiction to alcohol, a road accident, a broken engagement, and now cancer! I felt mean being angry and thinking these thoughts – I'd mostly believed in the intrinsic goodness of the Divine Spirit – but my reservoir had just run dry. I needed somebody with broad shoulders to hurl all my bitterness at, and what better target than God Himself.

Why Amma? It was a question I asked over and over again – baffled beyond belief. If ever there was one person who'd been through the grinder of mortal existence, it was her. Yet, her response to the Universe – grace, dignity, faith – had remained unchanged over the years. She'd stuck through everything in her forty-seven-year-old marriage with Appa – his alcoholism, loss of a job, four children to raise and finally the road accident that left him virtually bedridden after a series of hospitalizations.

My head filled with terrible images of the cancer eating away at her insides, causing her unspeakable suffering. I didn't have it in me to acknowledge a benevolent God right this minute. True to form, God – the strong, silent entity – continued to remain silent. I felt alone, helpless, adrift.

If I thought the phone call with my brother was challenging, speaking to Amma for the first time after she'd heard her diagnosis was heartbreaking. To hear her voice and know that she knew – even if she'd suspected something but ignored the symptoms – was agonizing. Across the thousands of miles that separated us, I was desperate to give her something to be happy about: I told her Mahesh was now in e-mail and phone contact with us all.

Her next words were proof of the grace and kindness still

shining through. 'At least, this situation has made him connect with all of you,' she said.

My heart squeezed in my chest.

'It didn't have to be this way,' I whispered, quickly cupping a palm over the mouthpiece so she wouldn't hear the wretched sobs that escaped my throat. I handed the phone to Girish who kept the conversation going until I'd put myself back together.

4

$\mathcal{T}$WO WEEKS AFTER WE'D ARRIVED IN CHICAGO, GIRISH AND I were already discussing possible dates for me to travel back to Chennai.

Amma had been Appa's primary caregiver for almost fifteen years now. Her cancer was a curveball none of us saw coming, caught up as we were in the complex management of Appa's delicate health.

Amma needed me. Appa needed me. So did Maya.

Between trips to Target, Walmart and IKEA to set up home, and organizing the details of Ruki's high school admission, we had our hands full. As our new lives took shape, our coffers steadily dwindled. A peak season ticket to India costs about $1,800. Mysteriously, an old business contact reconnected with me and a writing project landed in my lap. The cheque he wrote me for a proposal I generated was the exact amount we needed to buy my air ticket. God was working on my behalf – even as I turned my back on Him.

Mahesh and I took turns calling Maya and each other and compared notes. Next morning, he called with the latest update. Amma's bone scans were done. Thanks to inefficiency, miscommunication and inordinate delays, the procedure had taken an entire day at the hospital. Amma was in an awful lot of pain, but true to character, she'd been stoic.

I didn't know anything about bone scans; neither did I want to learn now.

Later that day my brother came over for a visit, arriving with a brick of vanilla ice-cream for Ruki. I was relieved he took the initiative because a) I didn't have a driver's license yet; and b) I knew my husband would jump through hoops for me, but I didn't want to subject him to the discomfiture that might ensue if he drove me to my brother's place.

Mahesh and I had met over coffee about seven months ago in Chennai on one of his visits, an attempt to iron things over. A pathetic, botched attempt, the conversation had degenerated into stock-taking of the worst kind – acts of omission and commission: Never a good recipe for reconciliation.

This time was different. There's nothing like a family crisis to glue the broken pieces together. There was no guarantee they'd stick forever, but we could function for now, even with all the cracks showing.

Over chilled beer and pizza, we shared our fears and uncertainties. Conversation zigzagged to his toddler, our new life in Chicagoland, school districts and driving lessons. It wasn't without its awkward moments, though. Like when he asked Ruki what grade she was in, and whether we were vegetarians. It was strange conversational terrain to navigate with one's own brother, evidence of how far we'd drifted from each other's lives.

We had to start all over.

It was hard to miss how my daughter and husband stiffened when he attempted a goodbye hug. All the acrimony of the silent years hung, unspoken, the air saturated with their weight. Being a remote uncle and brother-in-law is, clearly, not the same as being a brother.

All the mismatched moves notwithstanding, a huge part of me was comforted to have him back in my life.

5

*T*HREE WEEKS AFTER WE HAD ARRIVED IN CHICAGOLAND, I was on a British Airways flight back to Chennai.

Miracles abounded, beginning with my air ticket money. My in-laws were visiting from India and staying with my sister-in-law and her family in West Lafayette, Indiana. God had moved all the pieces just right in a grand cosmic connect. As my travel plans started to take shape, my in-laws cut short their stay in West Lafayette and arrived in Chicago three days before I was due to fly. Ruki was about to start summer school, and Girish had just started work in his new position, one that would keep him on the road for days.

Planning my trip provided a welcome distraction and as the days went by, I slowly emerged from the despair that had taken hold of me. Acceptance was slowly sinking in. I realized this was something that needed to go on God's to-do list; it was too complex for me to handle.

Leaving behind my husband and daughter soon after we'd started life in a new country was harder than I expected. If ever my fourteen-year-old needed her mother, it was now. She was about to set foot in an American high school classroom, a time of fears and insecurities, imagined and real. My husband was figuring out his new role, and the American freeway, chalking up hundreds of miles on his sales jaunts to Milwaukee, Indianapolis and Detroit.

Our furniture and household goods were still on a ship navigating the high seas. We were managing with the bare essentials, a kitchen cobbled together from my sister-in-law's kind donations and emergency supplies from Walmart. The ship would dock while I was in India; I'd miss out on setting up my home. Despite the mixed emotions the situation generated, there was no doubt in my mind that I needed to be in Chennai. I had to be there.

14 June 2008

Amma's cousin and his wife who had been holidaying in the US were coincidentally on the same flight. They were more than a little surprised to run into me, knowing how recently we'd moved. When I brought them up to speed about Amma's cancer, they looked visibly shocked and made polite enquiries. But it was hard to miss how they hastened to fill the air with conversation about our new life in Chicagoland, the city's infrastructure, and the adult children they'd been visiting. Our exchange flowed without a break and touched upon all things inconsequential just so we wouldn't have to deal with the dreaded C-word. I let it pass and chose not to question their intention. Most people are just plain uncomfortable when confronted with the tough truths of life.

On the first leg of the journey, I dozed, ate, people-watched and pondered life's uncertainties. Belted into my seat, I wondered whether Amma's physical appearance had changed in any way – pre-diagnosis, post-diagnosis. I knew Amma's first session of chemotherapy would be done before I arrived. Ignorant of what that involved – was it some kind of radiation therapy, would they inject something into her veins, was it a pill to swallow – I wasn't sure what to expect. All the movie actors who'd played cancer victims paraded before my eyes. Would she have lost weight? Would she have bags, lavender smudges under her eyes? Would chemo have damaged her in some way? A part of me was nervous.

Most of the flight, including the layover in London, was a blur. We touched down in Chennai right on schedule, 3.35 a.m. Somehow, the stark simplicity of Anna International Airport –

just two signs, Arrivals and Departures – was comforting after the glitzy maze that's O'Hare. I joined the line of Indian passport holders and was cleared in no time. However, a half-hour wait for my suitcase at the baggage carousel cancelled the time advantage I'd earned at immigration. Once again, I ran into the same relatives who enquired if I needed a ride home. I declined, knowing a taxi driver would be waiting outside, holding up a placard with my name on it.

Thin grey light streaked Chennai's dawn sky as I drove home. The taxi pulled up outside Seashore Apartments a little after five. I hefted my orange-coloured suitcase to the door, rang the bell twice. A stranger answered. Padma Mami, the recently-hired helper, as I learnt later.

Within seconds, Maya strolled out to greet me.

And there was Amma following behind, her eyes heavy with sleep, smiling and squinting into the bright glare of the living room tube light.

6

*A*mma wore a faded green nightie, the colours of her mussed waist-length hair an indication that her salon appointment was delayed. At 5'3" and 140 pounds, Amma was a small woman – her large dark eyes complemented her warm, welcoming smile.

A quick scrutiny and I zeroed in on Amma's 'puffy' eyes. A detail that once would've caused little concern now leapt out and worried me. When Amma disappeared into the kitchen for a minute, I turned to Maya.

'Her eyes,' I said. 'They're puffy.'

'Just sleepy eyes,' Maya was quick to assure me. Otherwise, Amma seemed her usual animated self. Defying Maya's orders to stay in bed, she was already filling me in on family news. We had a lot of ground to cover, considering I'd been gone for fifty-two days. She was getting an early start.

Appa got out of bed to say hello and give me a hug, then went back to sleep.

It energized me, Amma's positive spirit, made me swallow the woeful narrative I was about to launch into – about airline food and fellow passengers. Two hours had gone by when I finally managed to convince her to return to bed.

Maya and I have always talked up a storm. Our talk fests were legendary in the family. But once Amma was back in bed, Maya and I had to have the most difficult conversation of our lives. She brought me up to speed on everything – the discovery, the diagnosis and the several medical opinions. In all this time, she said,

Amma's composure had cracked just once. On the auto rickshaw ride home after the second doctor confirmed the seriousness of the diagnosis, she'd dropped her head into her hands and cried, 'Why me?' Tears sprang to my eyes, just hearing about it.

———⋘∘●∘●⋙———

The hearty meal Maya cooked – fresh white rice, broad beans, and a thick stew of coconut and sun-ripened mangoes – was the proverbial last straw in my resolution to stay awake. I fell like a giant oak and woke up four hours later, surrounded by darkness, and utterly disoriented. Maya told me the dark skies were because of a thunderstorm brewing on the horizon. The rest of the day was uneventful.

My parents lived in a two-bedroom ground-floor apartment with Maya and her husband, Guru. One bedroom belonged to my parents, the other to my sister and brother-in-law. I took the living room couch. It was almost midnight before I fell asleep again. This time too I only got four hours of sleep, because of my confused body clock. The rest of the household was still slumbering, so I picked up *Teacher Man*, the book I'd been reading on the flight.

An hour later, I decided to step out for a walk. Seashore Apartments was only five minutes from the ocean. I knew the beachfront would be jammed with an assortment of morning walkers – sari-and-sneaker clad women in their sixties, their dhoti-clad husbands in tow, young mothers eager to shed their post-pregnancy waistlines, forty-somethings desperate to regain their former youthful bodies, dog walkers, and the arthritic elderly who enjoyed the spectacle of a sunrise and the tactile pleasure of their prayer beads. It was a pearly morning, the air still and laden with moisture.

Girish, Ruki and I had lived in a condo just ten minutes away, and this beach was the place where people converged for their exercise. I set out, wanting to remain under the radar, not ready to run into someone I knew and answer a bunch of questions about why I was back so soon. I just wanted to be one of them for a while, out for a walk on a regular morning.

Forty-five minutes later, my sodden T-shirt clinging to my back, I decided to take a breather, my anonymity still intact. I sat on the embankment and fixed my gaze on the waves crashing on the shoreline: relentless, repetitive and rhythmic. I began to wonder about the cycles of nature and the cycles of life.

When I got to my feet and started the walk back home, I had the sinking realization that my cover was about to be blown. Approaching me from the opposite direction was a former neighbour. There was no way I could avoid him so I steeled myself, acknowledged the surprise on his face and gave him the bare bones of the situation, requesting him to keep it under wraps. I was not yet ready to have well-intentioned friends and acquaintances reach me via e-mail. The dreadful diagnosis would be less real if fewer people knew about it, talked about it, and discussed it.

I thought back to Maya's words. 'The oncologist says most patients know how serious it is; they just try to ignore it for as long as they can.' Amma had been concerned about toppling a couple of significant apple carts: Maya and Guru's wedding, a simple ceremony performed at home barely three months ago, and our move to the US. Perhaps, the most important in her eyes: Appa's fragile health.

———⋘∙∙∙⋙———

Amma's sixty-eighth birthday came around five days after my arrival in Chennai. I didn't know it at the time, but it would be her last. The previous evening, Maya and I had shopped for her gifts and returned with a pearl jewellery set and mushy, sentimental cards, as was our family custom. We got Appa to write a couple of lines on the cards too.

On her birthday, the phone didn't stop ringing all day: Amma's mother, brother, sister, sisters-in-law, niece, nephews, my brother and his wife. It was almost like everyone intuited there wasn't going to be another birthday, so they were determined to make this one the best ever. Her next-door neighbour visited with a handful of sweet-smelling jasmine and a heart full of warm wishes.

After talking it over, Maya and I decided to honour Amma's wishes on celebrating her special day. Amma was a foodie, but a restaurant outing was out of the question. Post-chemo, her immune system was compromised and we were taking no chances.

This year, she was very sure of what she wanted: a visit to the Krishna temple. Maya called a cab in the evening and we set off at half-past six.

A mild sense of panic gripped me as my bare feet touched the cool stone floor of the temple. It was both familiar and unfamiliar. The shaven-headed priests with their ash-smeared foreheads and Sanskrit chants had always felt like a wall between God and me. I focused on the black-stone deities adorned in the most gorgeous silks and ornate temple jewellery – bangles and nose studs, bracelets and waistbands, headpieces, chokers and brilliant glittering crowns.

A cocoon of sensations embraced me over the next thirty minutes: the air thick with incense and camphor, oil-soaked wicks glowing with the hopes of several devotees, wisps of smoke carrying their prayers heavenward. Upon request, the priest performed a special puja for Amma. I sat on the temple floor, the bhajans washing over me, a serenity taking over me. Everything was going to be good. Everything was going to be just fine. In the divine atmosphere of Amma's favourite Krishna temple, I felt certain that all those black-stone deities were on Amma's side – and mine.

7

AMMA'S FIRST MEDICAL REVIEW WAS THE DAY AFTER HER birthday. Amma, Maya and I rode a cab to Apollo Hospital. Amma carried a grey plastic folder, the lab results of her blood tests safely tucked inside. On the cab ride, I struggled to project a confident demeanour. Maya, adequately prepped by prior doctors' visits, scans, oncology department reviews and pronouncements, seemed inured to it now. She'd developed an invisible shield which I envied. My stomach did flip-flops as the cab pulled up to the hospital entrance. It was only now that the grim reality of Amma's prognosis began to rush at me.

The air inside reeked of disinfectant and despair. White-uniformed orderlies bustled about, carrying clipboards and file folders. People queued up at cash counters dispensing their hard-earned money with a prayer that it would be enough to save a mortally ill loved one. Others napped, catching precious moments of oblivion on thin, frayed sheets spread on the marble floor; some chewed on biscuits and vadas; while others noisily slurped sugary coffee from Styrofoam cups.

My first instinct was to turn around and flee – but that's not why I'd come all the way from Chicago. I sneaked a look at Amma, wondered what was going through her mind. She seemed composed, her fingers wound tight around the grey plastic folder. I stared at the folder, the hospital's name and logo embossed in blue.

We settled into the hard plastic chairs outside the doctor's cubicle. Thankfully, we didn't have to wait long, but it was the doctor's assistant who reviewed the test results. The doctor, I presumed, had more important things on his agenda than my mother's Stage 4 cancer. Ushered inside, we took our seats and stared at the young man's face as he looked over the reports, scrutinizing his features for an optimistic assessment.

Following her first chemo, Amma's white blood count had dropped to 6,000 from 10,300 – the normal range being 4,000–11,000. Her numbers were still reasonable, but he cautioned us that the count would drop further during week two, a time when she would be vulnerable to infection.

How on earth are we going to keep her safe?

8

$\mathcal{A}$S DAYS WENT BY, I CLAMBERED OUT OF JET LAG STUPOR and took small steps towards greasing the wheels of domestic administration. Interviewing a part-time cook was the most important task on hand.

Padma Mami, the interim helper, had been given the boot, because of her compulsive addiction to the living room television, a fondness for afternoon naps, and the barely passable quality of meals she dished up.

After consultations with an agency, we zeroed in on Vijaya Mami who arrived for the interview escorted by her grey-haired and starched-dhoti-clad husband. Deferentially positioned a foot behind the man she studied us, as we did her. It was hard not to like her. More importantly, I was certain Amma would like her.

Vijaya Mami was in her sixties, her cheery smile more appealing because of two missing front teeth. Gold studs sparkled on her earlobes, a diamond stud winked on her nose. On her wrists were red-and-green glass bangles that tinkled as she gestured. Her bearing announced a cultured background. It was evident the couple had fallen on hard times, with his retirement and the rising costs of living.

Mami's mild manner was her most endearing quality. A half hour later, there was happiness all around. Everyone was pleased with everyone, and the terms of employment. Mami offered to start work the following day.

She had been employed for just two days when she started a full-blown cold and began to sneeze-scatter her germs. Concerned for Amma's compromised immune system, I sent Mami home to rest, warning her to return only when she'd been fully cured of it. A day later, the cleaning lady's mother died unexpectedly and, understandably, she needed the week off. I rolled up my sleeves and set to work doing the laundry, dishes and meals, wilting in the soggy hundred-degree heat.

In the face of Amma's daunting health challenge, this was a no-brainer; the everyday tasks of normal living. But there were days when I wished I could open my mouth wide and let the screams rip. Between making a meal and cleaning the house, I would have to make half-a-dozen calls to the TV technician because Appa's TV, a.k.a. life support, was malfunctioning, and he yelled every three minutes to alternately complain and remind me. In the meantime, a technician from the washing machine company would show up with no prior appointment and as I explained the problem to him, the doorbell would ring again. The lab technician, this time, to do Amma's blood tests (we had to keep a constant eye on her blood count to make sure the levels remained within acceptable limits).

Amma was comfortable functioning in the middle of a maelstrom. The domestic situation in her house, even at the best of times, was disorderly. Amma chopped carrots and administered Appa's meds, her Zen attitude firmly in place. She navigated this frazzled, frustrating scenario – a calm oasis in crisis.

My life was driven by to-do lists and a reliable clock. There were days when I wanted to drop my head into my hands and weep, fight the impulse to flee. It took a chant to get *me* through those times, a mantra that preserved my sanity: *Amma needs me. Appa needs me. Maya needs me.*

9

$\mathcal{E}$VERY MORNING I ENGAGED IN A PRIVATE OBSESSION, RAKING Amma's hair with my eyes to see if it was beginning to thin or fall. And every day the evidence was to the contrary, my hopes were buoyed. I consoled myself with stories that her body was doing a great job of tolerating the chemo, that she'd be one of those who survived the regimen with her hair intact.

Two weeks after Amma started chemotherapy, my denial was cruelly shattered. Her hair started to fall.

I watched her standing in front of the mirror, her comb tangled in thick ugly knots inches above her scalp. As she yanked and tugged the comb free, a clump of hair dislodged and came away. The unspoken anxiety was palpable on her face: Will I lose all of it? I reassured her with lame words – 'hair is hair, it will grow back' – my words sounding hollow even to me. I felt a sinking sensation in the pit of my stomach.

She lost a lot of hair the following day. And she saved it.

Amma had started to grey in her twenties, but a former neighbour had introduced her to the wonders of hair colouring back in the early eighties when we lived in Hyderabad. Once Amma discovered how a bottle of artificial black softened her features and peeled years off her, there was no turning back. However, a zillion household responsibilities always got in the way of timely salon appointments, so her hair was mostly in varying stages of grey-black-reddish brown, until a family wedding looming on the horizon had her hotfooting it to the salon.

Five days after the hair fall started, Amma stopped combing her hair. Her constant scratching told me it was extremely itchy; a forest of angry knots a comb couldn't hope to traverse. I knew she was scared it would all come off if she tugged at it. This was her way of putting off the inevitable.

But here she was now, looking in the mirror and staring at the real possibility of a bald head.

10

RELATIVES AND FRIENDS STOPPED BY FREQUENTLY, BRINGING fruit baskets and health drinks, honouring the custom that you never visit someone's home empty-handed. Sometimes they stopped by in the middle of the day while Amma was napping. That's how it was in my town. People just dropped in informally. Calling to check on convenience is not common in a culture where receiving and serving guests is akin to serving God.

The relatives I ran into at O'Hare – Amma's cousin and wife – called on us one afternoon. Maya and I served them tea and engaged in conversation while Amma rested. They directed a volley of questions at us about the diagnosis, medicines, and her chemo regimen, but I was astounded that they skirted the topic when Amma eventually joined us. A striking contrast was another cousin, a cancer widow. Having lived through a personal loss, she had a natural ease around the subject, shared experiences, empathized and encouraged Amma's positive energy.

I'd been in Chennai two weeks already and missed Ruki and Girish, my homesickness marginally assuaged by phone calls and e-mails. On one such call, Girish's brusque tone bothered me, my mind spinning stories around it. He was monosyllabic and distant. When you're so far apart, it's difficult to stay in tune with each other. He had his own pressures: a slow start at work, shepherding Ruki through teen angst in an unfamiliar environment, adjusting to life in a new country. Usually I was around to cushion their collisions, but now he was challenged to draw deep from his dwindling well of patience.

I was still bristling from our cryptic exchange when the phone rang again. It was my husband. 'I'm sorry I was so short. It's just that ... there's so much happening. You took care of so much.'

That is all it took: the softening, the understanding, the validating.

'It's difficult,' he sighed, 'just staying on top of everything all the time.' After a pause, he added, 'I miss you in many small ways.'

It meant a lot. Reminders are so important.

It was the beginning of July. I knew I'd be back in Chicago by the end of the month. It felt like being split wide open, one half of me in Chicago, the other half in Chennai. There was always going to be a missing half.

11

DROPPING APPA OFF AT PAATI'S (MY MATERNAL grandmother), Amma, Maya and I drove to the hospital for her second review. This review was mandatory before her next chemo session, scheduled for the following day. The hospital would draw blood and also perform liver and renal tests, the results of which would determine the course of the chemotherapy regimen.

I'd been curious about Amma's oncologist, Dr R, for a while now. Maya had waxed eloquent about his happy vibe, sensitive radar and positive energy. Mustachioed and mild-mannered, Dr R was a lucky charm, or so I believed. When he directed pertinent questions at Amma, listened attentively, and encouraged faith in the treatment, I was sold.

Dr R smiled his well-perfected smile designed to reassure, comfort and soothe. 'She's doing well,' he said. 'Usually, it's the first chemo that causes all sorts of problems.'

I jumped in, enthusiasm on overdrive. 'Does this mean ... I mean, is this an indication that she'll tolerate all her cycles equally well?'

That smile again. 'It's like a One-Day cricket match,' he offered. 'Every game is a new game and so too every new chemo cycle.'

Chennai's humidity levels had been hovering between ninety-five and one hundred per cent. Always sensitive to moisture-laden air, Amma had caught a cold. Dr R put her on some anti-allergy medication and an antibiotic cover for good measure, hastening to assure us that a viral infection should in no way delay the chemo schedule.

My stomach tied itself up in knots. I sensed Amma's next question was coming, the one that kept her awake at night. She pointed to the mass of knots that covered her head – the matted hair of a saffron-clad sadhu. 'What to do?' she asked, searching the doctor's face.

I figured Dr R had been asked this question a gazillion times by cancer patients before Amma. His response instantly erased my previous impression of him. With an air of practiced insensitivity and a casual flick of the wrist he pronounced the solution. 'Shave it all off.'

I saw Amma's body stiffen at his suggestion, and the disgusting prospect of a shaven head.

Maya, Amma, and I had had the 'wig' conversation prior to the doctor visit. She'd agreed that investing in one might not be a bad idea, especially while there was still hair on her head: An umbrella for a rainy day, a wig for a family function.

On the way home, we stopped at a wig store. The young manager was patient, friendly and willingly answered our questions. 'We use pure human hair; synthetic hair is only used for celebrity wigs,' he explained.

He let Amma try on a black wig, fitting it snug around her head. Amma seemed satisfied with her reflection in the mirror. 'I look like I used to,' she said.

The man took her scalp measurements for a twenty-inch wig. 'It will cost 6,500 rupees,' he said.

That night, a friend, also a Reiki practitioner, offered to send Amma healing energy ahead of her second chemo session. Her instructions were clear. For the forty-minute session, Amma was to lie prone in bed, palms facing up and legs relaxed so her energy channels were open and receptive.

Appa's brain was unable to understand the ramifications of the word 'cancer'; in his simple mind, Amma was being treatment for an ailment. I explained the Reiki session to him as 'special prayers for her recovery', and cautioned him not to interrupt her for those forty minutes. He nodded sagely.

As soon as the session got underway, he gathered a pile of folded laundry from the foot of the bed and started to put it away, opening and shutting closet doors. It was his way of assisting her, lightening her load. It occurred to me when he turned on the television that this was like trying to meditate with a toddler in the room.

—<<•◦(•◦)•◦>>—

Back in Chicago, our earthly possessions had finally arrived, nine weeks after we moved. It meant hefting forty-three cartons to a second-floor apartment, unpacking them, finding the right niche for every item, clearing the debris and cleaning up. For me, it meant reading e-mail accounts of it while my in-laws, husband and daughter set up our home.

12

$\mathcal{S}$IX WEEKS HAD SPED BY AFTER AMMA'S INITIAL DIAGNOSIS.
E-mails were flying fast and furious between Chennai, Chicago
and Bahrain. Emotional seesawing was the order of the day.
When one was having a bad day, another reached out and lifted
spirits with an inspirational message, or a timely reminder of
earlier challenges overcome. It was a fine example of a family
safety net, each looking out for the other and maintaining the
sanity barometer for all.

Amma's second chemotherapy was scheduled for today,
exactly three weeks after her first.

This time, I alone would accompany her to the hospital; Maya
had an important meeting at work. After a restless night of tossing
and turning, I woke up early, an uneasiness snaking in the pit
of my belly. The fear of the unknown, the unexpected, and the
untoward coiled together. But I had to dig deep for reserves of
strength so Amma could feed off my positivity.

We left home at half-past seven, reaching the hospital forty
minutes later. Well in time for our appointment, we still had to
deal with the usual bureaucratic bungling that followed. The fifth-
floor staff sent us to the ground floor saying they needed a doctor's
consent form before chemotherapy could be administered; the
doctor was busy with a patient so we had to twiddle our thumbs
in the waiting room; when we finally saw him, he said the go-
ahead for chemo depended on Amma's blood test results, and the
lab had delayed the paperwork. Famous smile in place, he assured
us his assistant was on the phone to try and expedite matters.

'Will I tolerate the second cycle just as well as I did the first?' Amma voiced a question that must have kept her awake most of the night.

Dr R smiled genially. 'Some patients have a hard time with the first one, then go on to tolerate the following cycles better. Others sail through the first time. But generally patients who do well in their first cycle seem to continue that trend. But ...,' and he shrugged here, 'no guarantees. Alert us immediately in case of fever, vomiting, constipation, or diarrhea.'

All of a sudden, visions crowded my head: Amma doubled over, clutching her stomach, retching her insides out. Quickly, I shook my head free of the images and trained my focus on the doctor. Dr R wrote out a prescription for anti-nausea medicines, laxatives and a sedative.

Thirty minutes later, all the red-tape had been untangled. A deep sense of despair dogged me as the fifth-floor elevator doors slid open, and together, Amma and I approached the chemotherapy ward. This time, we produced the necessary documents, but all the beds were occupied.

'Wait outside,' the nurse said, waving a hand. 'We'll call you.'

Sighing, we stepped outside the ward to endure another long wait. It was a familiar hospital scene: a cluster of chairs; a side table with dated and dog-eared issues of *Sportstar, Woman's Era* and *India Today;* and people, listless, weary and waiting their turn. As was Amma's nature she was soon chatting them all up, patients and family members eagerly spilling their stories to her.

I listened to her conversation with a woman from Assam who spoke fragmented English. The woman shared that her fourteen-year-old son, a cancer patient, had already spent four months in hospital. Now he was looking at two more. Next, Amma turned her attention to a couple from Malaysia. They were in Chennai to celebrate their son's wedding when the groom's father had unexpectedly developed a crippling pain in his back. The diagnosis of pancreatic cancer had shattered their lives just two days before the wedding. His wife told us they were keeping the truth away from her elderly in-laws. Then there was a middle-aged man who'd accompanied his mother for a doctor's review. Months ago, he'd lied to her that her cancer was in the early stages and completely curable. The placebo theory had worked like a miracle. The woman had beaten Stage 3 cancer buying into the belief that her illness was indeed curable.

'She's in remission,' he told us, unable to hide the pride in his voice.

When it was Amma's turn to share her story, she declared 'breast cancer' without a hint of self-consciousness, as if it were a routine pink-eye or nose bleed. When you have a garrulous mother, you learn to retreat and save your words. Over the years, space and silence had become my defence against strangers, but this was Amma's podium. I watched her launch into the story of her diagnosis and treatment, demonstrating complete faith in the power of connection with fellow human beings.

During my growing years, she'd done this each time we moved to a new town and didn't know a soul. Using the simple tools of smile and small talk, she wormed her way into the hearts of some of the grittiest, crustiest people in the neighbourhood. Over time, the neighbourhood became a better place simply because Amma was in it, sharing her life, lentils and coffee powder with anyone who needed it.

Now, as everyone traded stories and strength, it occurred to me that all pain is the same. Each person brings a different shape and texture to it, but it is pain all the same. This was a club of believers trying to stay afloat on a rickety raft, not knowing what their life forecast looked like.

Finally, a bed became available. Before Amma went in, she had to sign yet another consent form which listed the possible side-effects of chemotherapy and absolved the hospital and staff, should untoward complications arise.

Pour that poison into my veins, and I promise not to hold you responsible if anything goes wrong.

It was half-past ten before Amma was comfortably settled and the IV drip started. The fourteen-year-old boy lay on the bed next to hers, an IV in his arm as well. I didn't know who to feel sorry for: my mother, the teenager, or myself.

Nurses and family members criss-crossed the cramped ward continuously.

Amma clutched an old copy of *Ananda Vikatan*, her favourite Tamil magazine, with its predictable staple of recipes, short stories, celebrity interviews, jokes and media gossip. Seeing that she needed an extra pillow for support, I moved to grab one from an unoccupied bed in the far corner. As I neared the bed, I spotted dirty black streaks on the side of the pillowcase. Flipping it over, I saw a large oil stain in the middle. It was all dragging me down.

Amma was feeling a bit chilly so I alerted a nurse who tipped off another who set off on a blanket-hunt from which she never returned. Fortunately, the first nurse was amenable to my suggestion that the window air-conditioner be turned off.

I stood on the side for a while and watched the IV deliver medicine into my mother's veins, trying to bolster my belief that this was the miracle drug that would save her life.

I waited outside the ward, popping in periodically to check on Amma. In the meantime, I also settled the doctor's fee and paid the bed charge at the outpatient cash counter, before stopping by the cafeteria for a tetrapack of grape juice. When I went back upstairs, Amma was fast asleep, the magazine splayed across her. It took about two hours for the IV bag to empty.

I clutched her hand and left the hospital in a hurry, not quite sure who need more comfort, she or I.

13

WHEN YOU GROW UP IN INDIA, YOU LEARN NEVER TO TAKE water and electricity for granted. In the easy way that we allow luxuries to slide into the category of necessities, a mere eight weeks in the US had skewed my perspective.

Back in Chennai, some mornings I woke up to an empty water tank. All bathroom routines depended on the arrival of the plumber whose ETA was a grand game of want-to-take-a-guess? Voltage fluctuations were common and fans whirred lazily, the ninety-five per cent humidity sapping our spirits. This also meant the laundry was on hold until power supply was normalized and the day's carefully planned agenda collapsed like a string of dominoes.

I had to calm down; remind myself that this had been my life for forty-three years. I was no spoilt diva.

In the midst of these everyday irritants the shadow of Amma's cancer loomed over us, powerful and threatening. When you're forced to confront something so epic, you realize how little control you really have. And because medicine doesn't equal a miracle, you turn that part of your brain off that questions, argues and debates the power of the unseen. For most of my life, I'd believed in a Higher Power, but I was far more cautious about toeing the cosmic line now.

The peaceful shrine of Velankanni Church had always been a powerful draw. Placing lit candles at the altar, I prayed with everything I had in me. The serenity of a church setting soothed me more than the clamour and commotion of a Hindu temple, but these days there was an urgency to my spirituality. When

Amma's neighbour handed me a small vial of holy oil, I grabbed it like the Holy Grail, fully trusting in its curative powers. At a friend's house, I dove into an evening of Sai bhajans in praise of Sai Baba – India's famous godman who materialized holy ash from the palm of his hand – and brought home vibhuti for Amma to smear on her forehead.

I trailed Amma like a faithful puppy; together we watched old Tamil movies and her favourite music shows on television. No matter what we did, the moments acquired a treasured quality in this season of her life, although I couldn't articulate why, with clarity.

At home, Amma stayed busy and engaged to the extent she could. She pottered around the kitchen adding the finishing touches to a meal, or offered Vijaya Mami a secret ingredient to enhance the appeal of a dish. I'd assumed responsibility for Appa's medicine reminders, and assorted tasks like topping up his bedside bottle of water, pressing his feet, and rubbing his back with an ayurvedic pain-reliever ointment he relied on to soothe stiff muscles.

In his mind, it was still Amma-on-demand; he hollered for her, expecting her to materialize. When I showed up, he morphed into a stubborn toddler testing his boundaries and insisted that Amma serve him. In spite of her children's collective protests, Amma continued to pander to Appa's every whim. She mashed his food and served him meals in bed – disregarding our assertion that Appa walk the few steps to the dining-table, a task he was perfectly capable of.

The love this woman's heart held for her husband – a man who had repeatedly challenged her sanity – was beyond comprehension, at least to us four kids who had grown up in the world of modern marriages and shorter fuses. Unmindful of the gravity of her physical condition, Amma continued to place Appa first. It was a love so pure, a love most of us can only aspire to.

Pampered by platinum-quality service, Appa paid little heed to me or Maya – the pathetic Amma substitutes. Unable to cure Amma of her devotion and eagerness to serve him, we eventually threw in the towel.

It was a win-win for both of them. Who were we to argue?

14

$\mathcal{T}$HIS WAS A CONVERSATION I'D BEEN DREADING, BUT IT WAS time. Amma's scalp was now bald in places; what was left of her hair clung to her head in ugly black knots.

'Amma,' I started, tentative and tense. 'Your hair ... what do you think of ... shall we get it done at Green Trends?'

'I don't want to go to Green Trends,' my mild-mannered mother responded with a determination that was completely out of character.

Green Trends was a salon right around the corner from Amma's house, a convenient location for an unpleasant job. Especially because Beauty & Grace – Amma's regular salon – was unwilling to handle the task of tonsure.

'Can I get it done ... here?' Amma's voice was soft, unsure.

'At home?'

She nodded.

'I can find out. Let me call them.'

I picked up the phone, pondering how to phrase my strange request, then decided against it. 'Actually, I'll just walk over and ask if they'll send someone home.'

My conversation with the manager at Green Trends did not get off to the best start. This was an unusual request, one they didn't often receive. After the initial hemming and hawing, she agreed to send a barber home, albeit at an exorbitant price. I didn't care. I was willing to do anything to protect Amma from the humiliation of a public tonsure. The heartbreaking scene played out in my head: a green-uniformed hairdresser wielding her clippers and snip-snip-snipping away while customers getting fancy perms and pedicures gawked shamelessly.

The day before the tonsure, my aunt called. Bag all your hair and save it, she told Amma. You can send the hair to Tirupati. All devotees who visited this holy shrine in southern India – male and female – made a special offering of their hair, a gift to the presiding deity.

Amma welcomed the suggestion as if it were divine intervention itself. I could tell it eased some of her anxiety surrounding the tonsure.

It's not that Amma had the best-looking head of hair in town, but it was *her* hair. Waist-length hair she'd nourished and nurtured with coconut and hibiscus oils, and adorned with sweet-smelling strings of jasmine. On auspicious festival days, she'd wash her hair before she embarked on an elaborate puja at her altar, convinced that the gods, impressed by her purity and piety, would double their blessings.

Gently, I unravelled the childhood memories tangled with Amma's hair: I saw the mother of my childhood emerge from the bathroom, her wet and fragrant hair wrapped in a soft white cotton *mundu* or towel. She'd finger-comb it first, run the wide-toothed side of the comb from top to bottom, air dry, and braid it. I loved to watch this ritual, lying on the couch. The flowers she tucked into her hair breathed the scents that perfumed our home.

I was not ready for this, the tonsure.

Hair is a woman's crowning glory. To Indian women, especially those that grew up in the 1940s and 1950s, hair often had the power to make or break a marriage deal. Many a marriage alliance had been sealed on the length, texture and beauty of a bride-to-be's hair.

There was a flip side to it, a significant truth of tradition I was conscious of. An Indian woman's head was only shaved when she became a widow. Growing up in conservative times, Amma, as a young girl, had witnessed the fate of other girls in their teens or early twenties whose husbands died of either snakebite or a fatal illness. It was real to her, the heartrending ceremony where these young girls were stripped of their bridal finery, clothed in widow's white, and their heads tonsured. Thankfully, education and the changing status of women have ensured the cruel custom is not as rampant; yet, for an Indian woman loss of hair comes with a clutch of negative connotations. I was aware that the superstition was a huge hurdle for Amma.

Knowing my mother as well as I did, it was easy to guess the one thought that would prey on her mind: what if Appa's health took a turn for the worse after her tonsure?

To a woman steeped in traditional values – as Amma was – this imminent head-shaving was a portent, one that foreboded a distinctly unpleasant outcome.

Amma chose to have the tonsure in the privacy of her bedroom, so I moved the beds around to create enough room. Next, I spread old newspaper sheets all over the tiled floor and set a chair in the middle. The power was off; the fans silent; the air inside the room, still and heavy. As I fanned her with a newspaper, the irony struck me: we were waiting for the hairdresser to arrive.

Appa had been temporarily shifted to the living room because she didn't want him to witness this act of indignity.

Minutes later, we were set: The three players – Amma, the barber, and I.

I tensed as I saw her body tremble, eyes shut tight, lips moving in silent prayer. It broke my heart, watching her work so hard at being brave. Tears stung my eyes, but I swallowed them, loath to cry. I needed to be the strong, supportive daughter.

The young man squirted a cloud of white foam and slathered it over her scalp with clinical detachment. Then, carefully using a blade he started to shave her hair off. Hair that had been lovingly groomed over sixty-eight years now fell to the floor in thick knotted clumps, a messy, foam-smothered heap. Parts of naked scalp began to emerge ... faster and faster, the hair fell ... and moments later, it was all gone.

Amma looked like a newborn. On the floor was dead hair.

The entire operation had lasted fifteen minutes, but they were the most torturous fifteen minutes of Amma's life.

I ran through a quick mental checklist, reviewed my aunt's instructions delivered over a phone call the previous night. Gathering Amma's hair off the newspaper sheets, I wrapped it in a sacred yellow cloth, slipped the cloth along with a one-rupee coin into a plastic bag. I placed the bag at the altar, under the watchful eyes of Amma's favourite deities. Next, I picked out a silk scarf, draped it over Amma's scalp and knotted it at the nape of her neck.

The hair-dresser gathered his kit and walked away after accepting a thick wad of rupee notes from me. When Amma and I stepped into the living room, we ran straight into Sarasu, the maid, who stopped dead in her tracks, her jaw dropping open with curiosity.

'Why are you wearing that on your head?' she asked Amma.

Amma didn't miss a beat. 'I'm taking some treatment. It's making my hair fall,' she replied.

From that moment on, Amma would never be caught without a scarf. Not even Maya or I were allowed to see her without her head-covering. Losing her hair was like an amputation; like losing an intimate part of herself. I could tell she never really recovered from it. Nevertheless, she smiled through it and never let it cramp her style, going out and meeting people.

The tonsure episode was still weighing on me a couple of hours later when the doorbell rang. It was Amma's neighbour, and another middle-aged woman she introduced as her cousin who visited homes and prayed for the troubled, the sick and the suffering.

'I told her about you,' she said to Amma. 'Can she pray over you?'

Amma, a believer in the spectrum that ranged from traditional Hindu rituals to anointed holy oils, ash and Christian Prayer Tower meetings, nodded assent without a moment's hesitation. We stood in a circle, holding hands. I'm not sure if it was the woman's prayerful voice or the words of supplication, but my face was soon wet with the tears I'd held in all morning. The mind tells us strange, comforting stories during times of stress. The one I was hearing right then was exactly what I needed to hear: this woman was a messenger sent to comfort and console. I needed reassurance and a promise that all was in divine order, and I'd just received it.

It was a rare moment of intimacy with God. One look at Amma, and I knew the same sentiments were travelling through her mind.

15

My RELATIONSHIP WITH GOD HAS TRAVELLED A ROCKY road for as long as I can remember. Unlike my siblings, cousins, and even friends, I was born a questioning brat with an enquiring mind – anathema in a culture where unquestioning obedience is a prized value. So I was usually shushed.

Fear was the dominant emotion I sensed in my parents and relatives when it came to religion, the driving force behind their connection to God. As for me, I had enough terror in my life – math exams, a raging alcoholic father, and the shame of being found out that I was the girl who had the crazy drunk dad. I certainly didn't need one more thing to be afraid of.

When we believe a monster lurks in the closet, we learn to leave that closet well enough alone. I stayed far away from the family altar. That's not so easy when you're growing up in a conservative Hindu family where every auspicious occasion has markers: rules, rites and rituals. On such days, I had to wash my hair, wear bangles on my wrist, a red dot on my forehead which is symbolic of the protective third eye, and starve until the gods had had their fill of the gastronomic delights especially prepared for the occasion. If I stepped out of line, the pantheon of gods, it was believed, would rain punishment upon me.

To every question I posed to my mother – Why must I wash my hair on an auspicious day? Why must I wear bangles before I light the lamp? Why can't I touch you before my bath? Her stock response was: 'We never asked questions. If an elder told us something, we simply obeyed.'

That didn't sit well with me. So, I pushed boundaries and tested people's patience. Often, I suffered the consequences – falling out of favour – and grew up with the disgraceful label of a rebel.

The gods of my childhood lived in a dark room, breathing in the fragrance of sandalwood incense. Photo frames of Saraswati, the goddess of learning; Hanuman, an incarnation of Lord Shiva; Lakshmi, the goddess of wealth; and Ganesha, the remover of obstacles, lined the puja room walls. Heavy perfumed smoke curled heavenward from slender midnight-blue joss sticks, ash threatening to crumble from the tips. Every time I sneaked a glance, I felt the eyes of the deities bore through the thin veil of my humanness, staring in disgust at the wrongdoings etched on my soul. I gave the avenger-punisher gods a wide berth, despairing of ever achieving the exalted status of near-perfection they demanded.

Every morning, Amma dotted the photo frames with wet sandal paste and vermilion, lit white squares of camphor and circled them thrice around each photo, muttering unintelligible Sanskrit chants. The smells of camphor, incense and burning wicks have stayed with me; the religious implications have not.

I was unable to transcend the dilemma. Appa swayed home drunk at night and the almighty gods turned a deaf ear to Amma's relentless pleas for his sobriety. There were other contradictions and double standards as well. Most of my relatives – regular chanters and faithful temple-goers – cast off their religious demeanour as easily as yesterday's clothes and indulged in, what seemed to me, completely irreligious behaviour in other areas of their lives. It was okay to gossip, tell little white lies, display superiority because you were born into a higher caste, and be unkind if someone didn't merit your kindness. When I held up the truth to the light, the elders blanched at my blasphemous utterances, shut me up and went about their lives. So, I did the only thing I could: I pushed this unjust God away from my life.

It was a nun in college who taught me psychology who

helped me find an anchor in god. Inspired by her devotion, and unwavering faith in the basic goodness of life, I started to spend more time in her company, hoping some of her optimism would rub off on me. She spoke of a loving god. God was a stranger in my world.

When she closed her eyes and prayed with everything in her being, Sister Valeria addressed god as 'Father'. I knew the 'Our Father' prayer, but I'd never really listened to it with my heart. I did now.

The words 'Our Father' were sweet melody to my ears now.

At a prayer meeting I attended, more out of curiosity than a desire for piety, I heard them refer to god as a *forgiving* father. Praying for the lonely, sick and bereaved, blessings were called upon all of them. All in plain, simple English, not a language that needed an interpreter.

For the first time in my entire life, a prayer sounded friendly.

It was incredible, this new vision of god I'd been granted: a loving, forgiving, understanding father. Such a contrast to my earthly father who unleashed a wave of shame and anger in me.

Sister Valeria's words spoken then continue to remind me of who I really am. 'You are God's statue, my child,' she used to say. 'He's sculpting and chiselling you and it hurts. But one day, a beautiful statue will come out of all this pain.'

My heart thawed enough to allow god into my life.

16

*I*T WAS MID-JULY, AND I'D BEEN IN CHENNAI A WHOLE MONTH.
Two weeks from now, I would be heading back to Chicago.

As time went by and Amma's treatment progressed, I turned
up the volume on my pleas to God. This took the form of temple
visits, completely uncharacteristic for me. I'd always preferred to
stay a safe distance from complex rituals, and slick, self-appointed
godmen.

But everything was different now. I was begging for my
mother's release from cancer-captivity. And I was ready to pull
out all the stops.

My maternal grandmother, Paati, was the family matriarch.
As far as I remember, Amma had always consulted her about
customs and rituals. Incurring her wrath was something no one
wanted to even consider. Honouring Paati's advice, Maya and I
visited the Marundeeswarar Temple one muggy evening. It had
been a five-minute walk from the condo I'd lived in less than three
months ago. I'd whizzed past it on my scooter a zillion times, but
had never before stepped over its threshold. Only now did the
significance of the temple's name – *marundu* (medicine), and
eashwaran (God), the god of medicine – really dawn on me.

In the presence of the glistening black stone deities and
oil-drenched wicks, my internal resistance to rites and rituals
melted away. The burnt fragrance and the rhythmic chanting of
shlokas awakened some dormant desire for a reconnection with
the Hindu in me. With closed eyes and a hopeful heart, I sent a
fervent prayer. *Please God, please just cure Amma.*

A few days later, Maya and I planned a surprise outing for

Amma and Appa. We kept the destination – Shirdi Sai Baba temple – a secret. The temple was an oasis of peace in the middle of a bustling roadway, the East Coast Road. A couple of kilometres into the drive and a few familiar landmarks later, Amma caught on. The radiance in her eyes glowing with joy at the prospect of a temple visit was ample reward.

Amma had always been drawn to spiritual abodes and practices. Her current health crisis had redoubled her pleas and prayers. She sipped 'blessed' water three times a day, rubbed holy oil all over her chest, bowed down low in front of her altar, and filled the house with her chants and shlokas first thing in the morning and last thing before she retired to bed at night. It's difficult not to be impressed by this degree of devotion. Even God, I was sure, had to relent.

A group of devotees were singing bhajans in the temple, their sweet voices rising and falling in mellifluous harmony, imbuing the night with a peaceful serenity. As we circled the courtyard at a sedate pace, one of Appa's sandal straps snapped. The ground was uneven and dusty, pebbles littered our path, there were many stairs to climb, but Appa was game. In the spirit of the true devotee, he literally propelled himself forward.

A half hour later as we were leaving the temple, I caught the look of supreme satisfaction on Amma and Appa's faces. In that moment I knew, this outing had been well worth the effort. For some families, picnics do it; for others, a movie and dinner is the flavour of togetherness. For us, at this point in our lives, a temple visit seemed most meaningful.

———<<·)●(·)●(·>>———

Every single day that I was with Amma, I made a conscious and mindful effort to ensure her happiness cup was full. I called a mobile library and got her a monthly subscription, so her favourite magazines would be delivered home. When I was out, I stopped by Higginbotham's and bought a stack of novellas by her favourite author, Sivasankari. Amma had, for years, been riveted by this author's domestic dramas: the tug between tradition and modernity, infidelity, life after loss and a woman's fight for self. Sivasankari became a familiar name to me when I was about eight or ten years old. The budding author in me must have been stirred by the magic this lady created, the way she kept my mother enthralled by the power of the written word.

Thirty-some years later, it was a proud moment for Amma when I was chosen from a large pool of writers to translate one of Sivasankari's novellas from Tamil to English. To my complete mortification, Amma told everyone she knew about this, using it as an inspiring introduction within new neighbours. Amma's facility in Tamil was impeccable because she'd studied the language even at college level, so I spent hours revising my drafts, with her guiding me to just the right word or phrase when I stumbled.

Although I'd lived only five minutes away from my parents before I moved to Chicago, my life, work and chores had kept me mired. Amma and I chatted every week, forty-five-minute conversations where she'd fill me in on everything from the latest newborns in the family to transfers, promotions, bridal trousseaus, and the quirks of her neighbour's visiting aunt. I checked in on my parents regularly, ran errands for them, and brought food for them, but something about this transatlantic visit was different. I guess it was that I stayed. I didn't leave at the end of the day to go back to my home, my bed. They had all of me; there were no distractions.

When news of her cancer first broke, I'd had neither the wisdom nor the perspective, but I saw it clearly now. God did have a purpose in all of this. My time with Amma, these six weeks, felt like a special gift, delivered straight from heaven. Watching the same soap operas I'd earlier yawned through, movies and music shows I hadn't cared for, Amma and I were filling a fresh bank of precious memories.

Even as I engaged in the simple chores of daily living – doing the dishes, hanging up the washing, chopping spinach, making coffee, and monitoring Appa's medicines – everything had new meaning. The finite end to my time here heightened my awareness, made me cherish the moments. When you're staring cancer in the face, you boil life down to moments.

⟨⟨●●●⟩⟩

A call from Girish always lifted my spirits, so when the phone rang and I heard his voice I greeted him with my usual enthusiasm. As the seconds ticked by and he talked, my spirits plummeted until all the good feelings crashed and shattered around me. Long story short: his company was sending him to Thailand on a week-long business trip, and he was flying out the same day I was due to arrive in Chicago.

This wasn't the reunion story I'd been fantasizing about. I quickly went from angry, resentful mode to a super sulk followed by a pity party. Over the next couple of hours, I took stock and dialled down my emotional barometer to a dull resignation. It was the best I could do. In trying to find a solution, he'd suggested that I advance my arrival by a few days but something about that didn't resonate with me. I had committed these six weeks to Amma, and I wasn't going to cheat either one of us out of a single moment. I decided not to reschedule my ticket, just tried to get used to the idea that I'd be seeing him after seven weeks instead of six.

Mahesh was also going to be away on a business trip. The fact that he called the next day and gave me the number of a reliable taxi service meant the world to me. It was heartening to know how deeply my brother cared, even after all these years of bitterness that had shut us off from each other.

17

FOUR DAYS BEFORE I WAS DUE TO FLY BACK TO CHICAGO, MY sister Vidu and four-year-old nephew, Abu, arrived in Chennai. I was handing the baton to her – she would spend the next five weeks with Amma. I was delighted to see them and a tad disappointed that our time together was going to be so short. On the bright side, my leaving meant more closet space and elbow room for them.

It took us back to our childhood, four children in the six to twelve age range, two parents and a grandma living in a two-bedroom, one-bathroom apartment. We were no strangers to living in claustrophobic spaces. The four of us and Thaathi (my paternal grandmother) used to sleep on thin mattresses spread out on the living room floor, the scary darkness offset by Thaathi's soothing voice as she told us stories from the great Hindu epics, the Ramayana and the Mahabharata.

Now that all four of us siblings were married and had neat, orderly lives in our large homes, the space restriction at my parents' place crowded in on us. It bothered us; the higgledy-piggledy of towels and skirts draped on furniture, the long wait for the bathroom (someone was always there), and trying to sleep when someone else was having a meal. Fewer rooms and more people meant the living area became a multi-purpose space. We ate, slept and hung out just about everywhere.

Even so, we laughed about it and took it in stride, just happy to have each other – the extra shoulders to lean and cry on.

What we failed to factor in was the cleaning woman's perspective on this. With a full house, her motivation instantly nosedived. I imagine she told herself that many hands make light work. So she decided to take the day off with no advance warning, then the entire week off. Vidu and I had no choice but to roll up our sleeves and get busy.

We tried to cook meals which Amma would enjoy, but that was short-lived. The most notable side-effect of Amma's chemo was the mouth sores she was starting to develop. Even the mildest diet of cold yogurt mixed into white rice caused her acute discomfort. Watching her hiss and become teary-eyed through every meal was painful. I could barely taste my meal, watching her struggle to finish the tiny portion of food on her plate.

Abu, with his natural ability to distract Amma from all the angst surrounding her illness, was a blessing.

Abu was born with a competitive gene. One evening, a friend of mine was visiting with her husband and teenage daughter, Shloka. Shloka engaged Abu in a board game that involved racing cars. No matter what the outcome, Abu insisted on declaring himself the winner every time, on occasion shouting. 'I'm the winner,' well before the game had begun. My friend tried a ploy at changing Abu's perspective. 'The game will only have one winner, but the loser gets the prize,' she said. The next time Abu declared himself the winner, my friend said, 'Okay. Shloka gets the prize,' to which he protested loudly. It was a silly game, but we all ended up laughing a lot, especially Amma.

Over the next couple of days the house was buzzing with friends and relatives dropping in to say goodbye before my departure. If four days with Vidu felt too short, so did six weeks with Maya. There was always more talk left at the end of little time.

My in-laws, who were holding the fort in Chicago, were getting ready to fly back to India. In less than a month, Ruki would begin her sophomore year at William Fremd High School. It was time for me to turn my attention homeward, even if that word caused a momentary flicker of confusion inside me. Amma's home was 'home'; our own condo in Chennai was 'home'; and now, so was our Schaumburg apartment.

My last night in Chennai, Amma and I were sitting on her bed. Overcome by a moment of intense emotion, I held her tight and whispered, 'I don't want to leave you and go.'

'It's time for you to go,' she said, patting my back. 'Girish and Ruki are waiting for you. They need you.' And then she smiled her gentle smile, her eyes brimming with kindness.

We three sisters stayed up talking well past midnight while hyperactive Abu leapt off the living room divan and dove into the mattresses on the floor, messing up the sheets and making his mamma mad.

Maya's alarm rang at quarter to four in the morning.

I got out of bed, got dressed and was cramming last-minute stuff into my bulging suitcase when the taxi arrived. Amma got up to answer the front doorbell. I suggested that she not wake Appa, but she insisted he'd be upset if I left without saying goodbye.

As was the custom, I got down on my knees before Amma and Appa, bent down low and touched my forehead to the floor and their feet. Placing their palms on my head, both whispered a blessing. Amma pressed a firm kiss on my cheek. Maya and Vidu hugged me tight while Abu slept on unaware of the goodbyes and miss yous being exchanged.

The driver loaded my bags in the boot. I settled into the seat, the neighbourhood deep in the slumber of dawn, a thin light leaking in to wake up the sky. I looked out of the taxi's window and waved.

Amma stood in the doorway, a pink scarf draped around her head, the sharp outline of her cheekbones evidence of her recent weight loss. As she lifted her hand in a wave, the taxi started to move, eased its way out of the gates of Seashore Apartments.

I didn't know it then, but that was the last time I would see Amma alive.

18

$\mathcal{I}$ was full of mixed emotions flying home to Chicago after spending six weeks with Amma. Home had come to have a fragmented meaning. I remembered how I paused as I said the words to Amma as a new bride – 'I'm going home' – meaning my new married home. Home had always been where Amma was. So while I was happy now to be going home to my husband and daughter – I'd missed them terribly – a part of me was nervous about how Amma's story was going to turn out.

On the last leg of the journey, I struck up a conversation with my fellow passenger, Anne, who was returning to her hometown in Michigan after a six-month stint teaching English in Istanbul. I told her I'd been a freelance trainer with the British Council in Chennai, teaching Business English to technically-skilled but linguistically-challenged employees in the IT sector. Anne gave me a ton of useful information on job search opportunities in Chicago.

At O'Hare, my overweight suitcase posed a real problem at the baggage carousel. Struggling to haul it off and failing, I watched haplessly as it went round the conveyor belt a second time when Anne popped out of nowhere, grabbed it like it was a bag of fruit and wheeled it towards me, a big grin on her face.

She's my angel. God is looking out for me, for all of us.

As soon as I came through the Green Channel and Exit gate I scanned the area, anxious to spot Girish and Ruki. The bobbing head of silver by the information desk was my husband, and there was Ruki, right beside him. I practically ran towards them, my suitcase groaning as it followed me.

I was home!

Girish's flight to Thailand was due to take off in a half hour; a friend was giving us a ride home. We had ten precious minutes with each other; my talk-a-thon simply had to be put on hold. However, feeling his arms around me and smelling his aftershave felt like the best homecoming.

As soon as Ruki and I got home, my daughter who usually rationed her words began to talk non-stop about her summer school experiences: the courses she was taking, books she'd read, and life in America. It was obvious she'd missed me.

I wandered around the apartment that had been set up by my in-laws, husband, and daughter. A flat screen TV occupied pride of place in the living room and it was comforting to see all our Chennai furniture in a new setting, sitting on an expanse of carpet instead of mosaic-tiled floor.

Ruki nattered on, my self-appointed tour guide.

I felt like a stranger in my own home, asking Ruki where I might find the sugar bowl and coffee.

Desperate to wash off airline grime, I stepped into the shower. As hot needles of water pounded my stiff muscles, I felt an unspeakable guilt wash over me. This was a simple pleasure that Amma was denied back in Chennai. I thought of how she'd stand in the bathroom every morning and fiddle with the knobs, squinting up at the indoor tank, praying for the day's supply of water.

An hour later, pulling the comforter up to my chin, I realized how happy I was to be back. Ruki was lying beside me, insisting she still had so much to say. She talked and I talked, and she talked some more, and I talked and she continued to talk, and I became monosyllabic as my eyelids grew heavy. At some point she must have stopped talking, the point when her questions were answered by gentle snores.

19

*I*N EARLY AUGUST, MAYA CALLED TO SAY THAT AMMA'S oncologist had recommended three more cycles of chemotherapy. I wrote her an e-mail later that day. '... almost everyone we know needed in excess of three cycles of chemo to beat this ... we cannot and must not give up ... cancer is not easy on the patient or the family ... we have to fight it with all we've got ... and we will.'

As I wondered about Amma's thoughts on another round of chemo, Mahesh called. He'd talked with Amma, he said. In her words, 'I've taken it well; I'm not disappointed. The doctor says I'm responding well to the chemo.'

Around mid-August, Maya's landlord, whose primary mission in life, it appeared, was to sabotage his tenant's well-being, delivered an ultimatum: pay a rental increase, or find another place to stay. Given the man's reputation, Maya believed moving was the better alternative. Two ill parents, however, made for a tricky situation. Finances were also a key consideration in the choice of apartment. Besides, twenty-four-hour water supply and an elevator – amenities which people in developed countries take for granted – many times belong in the category of luxuries in India. My spirits took a beating once again. Frustration, anger and turmoil coalesced inside me. *I'm not in Chennai when they need me the most. I could've taken on the responsibility of apartment-hunting.*

Unexpectedly, it was Mahesh who came to the rescue. His virtually brand-new three-bedroom apartment in Chennai had remained locked up since he'd relocated to the US. Why not consider moving there? When he initiated the idea, it seemed like the perfect solution.

Again, I chose to focus on the bright side of things. It looked as if all the puzzle pieces were finally coming together.

———◄ ♦◖ ◖♦ ►———

Now that I was back in Chicago, it was time to take the test and get my driver's license.

In the three weeks that Girish, Ruki and I had stayed with my sister-in-law's family in West Lafayette, I'd taken a few driving lessons with a private instructor. As the written test deadline loomed, and pressure from my husband grew, I pored over the Illinois driver's manual like my life depended on passing it. Thankfully, I aced it. Over the next couple of months, I practiced parking, turns and driving at different speed limits in and around the Schaumburg area.

Reflecting on my life, it's evident that experiences most people embrace at an early age have been brought to me much later. I learnt how to swim at the age of thirty-five; I rode a scooter for the first time at thirty-six; and I was now learning to drive at forty-four. That also explains why I didn't approach any of those activities with the exuberant free-spirited joy that a teen would. Loads of trepidation and a knotted stomach were my reality.

Ruki dove into high school life with gusto. She bravely auditioned for her first musical ever – *Bye-Bye Birdie* – but was not cast. Undaunted, she landed a spot on set crew, and from there on, was involved in every high school production, be it as an actor, crew member, assistant director, or stage manager. Theatre has always been pure joy for her. It was exciting to watch her blend seamlessly into an alien culture, even if her constant crooning of those musical numbers drove me crazy.

Slowly, the three of us settled into a routine. Girish spent more hours on the American freeways than he did at home, his job taking him to Indianapolis, Milwaukee and Cincinnati. I spent hours in front of my laptop searching for a suitable position in the area of teaching English as a Second Language (ESL) to immigrant adults. I took a few courses to gain the right certifications, unprepared for the common response I encountered: my Cambridge University certification and experience as a British Council trainer in India counted for nothing. It didn't help matters that our move to America coincided perfectly with an economy in freefall. Opting for a wider playing field, I applied for a variety of jobs – administrative, clerical, receptionist – but heard from nobody.

Vidu's Chennai stint wound down; she and Abu flew back to Bahrain in early September. By this time, Amma had undergone six cycles of chemotherapy and continued to remain stable. After the sixth cycle, and during the end-September medical review, Dr R was pleased with her progress. 'I've seen people struggle. I'm amazed at the way you have tolerated chemo,' he said. 'You have not reported any major difficulties and you are going about your normal work.' But as a safety measure, he recommended thirty-two sessions of radiation therapy – six weekly hospital trips.

Thirty-two sessions of radiation!? I wondered what that would involve?

The cancer treatments seemed never-ending, and Amma's side-effects – mouth sores and fatigue – were taking a toll on all of us. Yet Amma continued to remain cheerful. 'You have to go through whatever you have to,' was her stoic response. Her faith in a Higher Force was unwavering.

In September, Mahesh and his wife invited us to dinner at their Naperville home. It was a very pleasant evening of bonding over a delicious meal, and we enjoyed a lot of laughs at my nephew's non-stop chatter. When Ruki, who's partial to toddlers, pronounced, 'I have two cute cousins now,' I felt a warm glow wash over me.

Meanwhile, Mahesh was negotiating a leave of absence at work to travel to Chennai. If the dates worked out, part of his stay would overlap with the time Maya was going to be out of town on a month-long training programme. All the cards were lining up neatly.

It was October when Mahesh travelled to Chennai for a three-week stay. His time there was not without the usual rumbles that accompany my brother's presence around immediate family. I have come to realize that this is usually the case when conflicts are unresolved. They continue to simmer below the skin, bubbling to the surface at the slightest provocation. Nevertheless, the details of the move to his apartment and a timeline – January 2009 – were finalized.

Amma was happy to have Mahesh home. The timing was perfect: she was between chemotherapy and radiation. The reprieve came right in the middle of Diwali, the festival of lights. Family, food, shopping, and firecrackers make up the merriment in what was Amma's favourite festival. The festival's theme of the triumph of good over evil has long since been drowned out by the consumerist commercialization of the century – as happens with most celebrations worldwide. Even so, it's a season Indians look forward to – all about family connections, fireworks lighting up the night sky, candles and oil-lamps illuminating doorways and window-sills, and shopping for new outfits.

Amma always started her Diwali preparations well in advance. She'd make long lists: goodies to order and share with family, neighbours and household help; decorating the home; and sweetmeats she'd make from scratch right in her kitchen. I imagined this year was even more special and wished I could be with her. A celebration was in order after the gruelling five months of treatment she had endured. It would offer her a chance to shift her attention to the pleasure of festivity. For now, knowing she was in a healthy place and had her son around was enough cause for joy.

20

$\mathcal{B}$ACK IN CHICAGO, THE THREE OF US WERE SETTLING DOWN. Every so often, we treated ourselves to little slices of history and sightseeing – the museums, Navy Pier, the architectural cruise, and parks. But on every phone call to Chennai, I stopped short of sharing my fun experiences. Guilt threatened to swamp me. How could I possibly gush about an architectural cruise on Lake Michigan when Maya was updating me on Amma's mouth sores and medicine doses?

I confessed my confusion to Girish whose perspective helped me feel modestly better. 'Are you going to help yourself or anyone in Chennai by being miserable? By denying yourself these simple pleasures? Amma would want you to be happy, don't you think?'

It was difficult to argue with that.

Waiting to land a job with the economy in freefall, I decided to use my time to volunteer as an ESL tutor at the Schaumburg Library's 'Read-to-Learn' programme. We only had one car, our Corolla which Girish drove to work, so I rode the Pace Dial-A-Ride bus to the library.

One afternoon, waiting for the bus at the library, I spotted tiny white confetti falling from the sky. *Dandruff from the sky,* was my first thought before the word *snow* registered in my brain. And then it hit me. *Snow flurries.* I'd learnt the words from Tom Skilling and the *Chicago Tribune* and here I was, having my first experience of it. I stood there savouring the magical sight, my nose pressed to the cold glass pane, my heart pounding with excitement.

As soon as I snapped out of the spell, I grabbed my cell phone and stepped out to call Girish. 'It's snowing! Go outside! It's just like those pictures on the cards we received in India!' Passersby threw crazy glances my way. A forty-something woman behaving like an excited toddler! I *was* that forty-something woman experiencing her first snow. The only other time I'd seen snow was on the distant peaks of the Himalayas, the morning sun sparkling on a vast expanse of white, white icing on a chocolate cake.

Our first-ever Thanksgiving was in West Lafayette, with Girish's sister and family. Driving back to Chicago, everywhere we looked there were mounds of snow. I couldn't stop gazing at it, talking and exclaiming about it even as hardened Chicagoans squelched my child-like enthusiasm: *We'll give you a month to get over it. Wait till you drive in it. By March, you'll want to cry when you see snow.* I pooh-poohed them all. For now, snow was magical to me and I revelled in the thrill of big, fat flakes falling in silent whispers from the sky. Coming as I did from a country where the coolest was a seventies day, this felt like living right in the middle of the Arctic. Or like living in the Christmas picture postcards we received from friends who lived in this part of the world.

⟨ ⟩

Amma started radiation treatment in November. To make her hospital trips less painful, Girish arranged a chauffeured car via his Chennai office. Friends and family – cousins, sisters-in-law and sister – all chipped in, taking turns to accompany her until her thirty-two sessions of radiation were done.

Before leaving on her trip, Maya had called a home help agency and hired a live-in. Sarasu, a young girl of sixteen, moved in and learnt the ropes so quickly she became an integral part of the household. With her quick wit, indefatigable energy, and a willingness to learn, Sarasu endeared herself to Amma, Appa and Mahesh in record time.

In a rare moment of despair, the young girl had confessed the sordid details of her life story to Amma. Her father, a drunk, lived with another woman, but barged into their home, beat Sarasu's mother and stole the young girl's hard-earned money.

An endless reservoir of positivity, Amma consoled the girl. 'Put your faith in God. He will definitely reform your father. Your family *will* see better times.' When Mahesh told me this story, the truth struck home in a fresh way. Innate optimism had been Amma's biggest ally, shepherding her through the dark, depressing days of Appa's alcoholism, road accident and endless hospitalizations. Nothing shook her belief in the reality of a day when he would turn into a sober, responsible man and take over the family reins. And she did have her wish. For eight whole years – before the accident reduced him to a child-like state – Appa had rediscovered his loving, responsible self, a wonderful husband and caring father. From the position of believer, Amma now fed the same optimism to Sarasu.

21

$\mathcal{I}$ KEPT UP THE JOB HUNT, RELENTLESSLY E-MAILED applications for a variety of positions. As the silence grew louder, my confidence and optimism began to dwindle.

Weeks later, my application to Test of English for International Communication (TOEIC) was the only one that had elicited a response. I was elated, even if the formal communication was just the beginning of a long process. TOEIC is an organization that uses global testing standards to assess English proficiency for business. They were looking to hire testers who would grade reading, writing, listening and speaking tests to measure the ability of non-native speakers of English to succeed at the workplace.

To me, the opportunity was a godsend. The position was tailor-made for me, considering my last two years in India had been spent training and assessing IT professionals on the exact same skills.

However, TOEIC didn't bother too much with credentials, but required every applicant to take a sample grading test to prove their skill level. You didn't *have* to pass the test on the first try. An applicant could take the test a total of three times, and would, on passing it, be appointed a tester.

In my mind, the test was a mere formality. I was a certain hire. TOEIC had e-mailed me documents to study in preparation for the test. Then, I had to grade the speaking and listening tests before returning them to TOEIC. I went to work right away: I reviewed the material, made notes and revised.

Next morning, anticipation pulsing through my veins, I took the test … and failed! After the initial jolt, I laughed it off. *I must have missed something silly.* More attentive, I trawled through the course material again. I took the test a second and third time … and failed all three times!

I stared at my laptop astounded, the words on TOEIC's e-mail exploding all over my brain: '*… you have not been chosen … failed the test three times … please know that you can try again after one year has passed …*'

When Girish returned home from work, I was still in shock.

'So, what happened?' he asked, fully expecting to hear that I'd aced the test and was soon to receive my employment confirmation.

'I … I don't know how …'

All I could do was lay my head on his shoulder and weep tears of frustration.

As he stroked my hair and shushed me, the words I had never planned to speak spilled from my lips. 'I don't understand why this is happening, but when God closes a door, He opens a window somewhere.'

I had no idea why I was saying this, because all I could feel and hear at this moment were doors slamming shut. And yet, some tiny sliver of space in my heart believed in those words.

Back to the drawing-board, I dove into the application frenzy.

A few days later, I had another lucky break: a part-time job. The position invited applications from people who wished to teach basic computer skills to residents in a senior-living community. That level of technology I could handle, but one word on the advertisement leapt out at me: memoir. Helping the elderly write their life stories was part of the job description. I hadn't the foggiest idea what made the senior population in this culture tick, but if the elderly here were like those where I came from, it wouldn't take too much persuasion to get them to tell their stories.

My interview was in the third week of December. I crossed every finger and every toe, hoping and praying nothing would trip me up this time. As it turned out, the interview was a formality. A three-hour orientation programme was next.

The company that hired me was partnering with a well-known senior living corporate to launch the programme in a series of retirement communities. In a nutshell, the programme – Connect 101 – was about using technology to connect seniors with their community, family and the world at large.

Computer labs were going to be set up in every building. Hires like me would work with the seniors one-on-one, teach them how to send and receive e-mails, upload photos, play games and write their life stories. As a concept, it was a sure winner, combining the elements of entertainment, communication, legacy and connection. All of which totaled up to deliver the grand prize: better brain health.

22

$\mathcal{D}$ECEMBER WAS ON ITS WAY OUT WHEN I STARTED MY PART-time job at The Palms.

When I first stepped inside the building, I thought I'd strayed into a five-star hotel by accident. The spit and polish of the place struck me dumb. The glittering chandeliers, rich carpets in the hallways, well-stocked library, game room, pool table, art studio, dining hall and eight floors of residential apartments just about knocked me over. As I toured the building with the executive director, I had to constantly remind myself not to gape.

A surprising moment presented itself as we strolled down the corridor in the lower level of the building. My eyes lighted on a small sign: BEAUTY SHOP. What a beauty shop is doing in the basement of a building that houses eighty- and ninety-year-olds, I wondered: More a genuine query and less of a judgment.

In my culture, grandmas and grandpas are part of the regular family unit. Retirement communities are frowned upon and certainly not the favoured choice. To send one's aged parents to such a facility implies that you don't take care of your own. I'm fairly certain the day is not too far off when India will go the way of the Western world in that respect too. The process is well underway with McDonald's and the magnificent mall culture.

At the present time, however, prayer beads and temple visits are the reality of seniors in my culture. The twilight years of life, they believe, are about detachment and renunciation. Life is more about embracing a higher consciousness and less about the self.

That being my reality, the glitz and glamour of a Western world retirement community was completely new territory. Little did

I know that beauty and grooming were dominant to-dos in the daily life of an octogenarian. That perms and pink nail polish, manicures and mascara were still carefully balanced with doctor's appointments and dental visits. Neither of my grandmas even knew what the inside of a beauty salon looked like. If you mentioned the word mascara, they could be pardoned for thinking you were referring to a disease. A part of me thought: *vanity doesn't age here.* Another part was full of admiration that seniors here still cared about cosmetics and colour-coordinated clothes.

The Palms was so cavernous it took a whole week to orient myself geographically.

While computers were being installed in the seventh floor lab, I had to make do with the clunky old model that sat in the game room.

Ninety-six-year-old Frances was my first one-on-one. A frail, silver-haired lady who dressed impeccably, Fran was a real darling. That someone so old was willing to face a computer screen came as a welcome surprise to me.

My company had designed a senior-friendly portal, complete with big, bright easy-to-click icons and bold fonts. I'd called Fran's daughter the previous day to get hold of family e-mail addresses. As we got started on the tutorial, I described to Fran how quickly an e-mail could travel from where we sat to her great granddaughter, Nicole.

Fran listened, her eyes growing wide, like a child watching a sorcerer's tricks. Then she asked me with all the innocent wonder of a three-year-old, 'You mean to say we don't need stamps!?'

Trying to keep the lingo simple, I explained that her e-mail message would travel from this computer and drop into her great granddaughter's virtual mailbox. 'Oh my goodness! That's like magic!' Fran exclaimed, clapping her hands.

Right then, I knew this was going to be a fun job, but more importantly, a meaningful one in helping lonesome elders build bridges to family members they didn't see too often.

As we chatted, an e-mail message dropped into Fran's inbox. It was from her great-granddaughter,, thrilled to be connected with her great-grandma 'Congratulations, Gram! You're on e-mail, how cool!' read the message.

By now, Fran really believed we'd been teleported to a fantasy land where normal, everyday rules like envelopes and mailmen did not apply. Watching the experience through Fran's eyes gave me a whole new appreciation for technology. In a life stage underscored by the pain of loneliness, a computer could actually foster human connection.

A great grandma and her great-granddaughter had just bonded in the most poignant way across the many miles that stretched between them.

❖❖❖

Ruki's first-ever high school musical, *Bye-Bye Birdie,* was a huge success. At the end of the show, a couple of her drama teachers chatted with us and extolled her work ethic. Ruki was, undoubtedly, the heroine of our move. The manner in which she'd grabbed hold of the opportunity with both hands made it so worth it.

Ruki had an ardent champion in her grandma. Amma had always been proud of her granddaughter's tremendous potential. May be Amma had been driven by exactly this motive in keeping her cancer a secret until we'd arrived in Chicago.

23

*I*T WAS A SLOW START AT WORK, ONLY A FEW HOURS A DAY. The company being a start-up and the new computers still to arrive, I spent most of my time befriending the seniors and advertising our programme, Connect 101. I found myself on a remarkable learning curve. One of my earliest lessons growing up was – respect your elders, no matter what. This translated into no answering back or arguing or questioning when instructed by an elder. It was a time-tested rule of tradition, one we were expected to honour. Raging teen hormones and figuring out self-identity just didn't cut it as excuses.

The respect rule also meant you sprang to your feet like a scalded cat and offered your seat if you spotted an elder on the bus, or in a crowded room. You carried their groceries, offered a shoulder for them to lean on, and touched their feet to receive their blessings for everything from a math test to a marriage proposal.

Faithful to my upbringing, I applied the same rules here, but was totally unprepared for the resistance and even resentment I encountered from seniors. It took me several weeks to figure out that, of the most-valued traits in this part of the world, independence topped the list. Seniors living in retirement communities had to contend with the loss of independence and now needed to submit to a degree of caretaking. A huge blow to their self-esteem, as I later learnt. This culture celebrated the 'self'; where I came from, 'community' was the focus. In the Eastern culture, key decisions in life – a job offer, a geographical move, investing in a new house, a wedding – were rarely taken without consulting family elders and seeking their blessings. And if grandpa or great-granduncle had a serious reservation, you listened carefully and considered it because it was the voice of wisdom talking.

In America, my innocent action of rescuing a cane a senior had accidentally dropped, or extending a hand when their steps faltered was an affront to their sense of independence. Much of it had been taken away already. They'd had to give up homes they'd lived in for forty, sometimes fifty years, and move into community living: a loud declaration of dependence. My intentions to assist them seemed as spicy and unpalatable as Indian curry.

Slowly I began to integrate, one step, one lesson at a time.

⟨⟨≫≪⟩⟩

I'd been working in the building three weeks when news of my mother's passing toppled my world. I called my supervisor, Lori, and informed her that I was getting on a plane to India. However, I forgot to call Fran and cancel our upcoming appointment. She called home, Girish later told me, and was very upset to learn of Amma's passing and my sudden travel.

I didn't realize it at the time, but in losing my mother I would become a daughter to many others in a new country.

Two

January 2009 – January 2011

1

$\mathcal{I}$T IS TWO HOURS AFTER I RECEIVED THE TERRIBLE NEWS that Amma is gone, a time of bottomless sorrow.

Girish is driving home to me. On the drive, he sets up a three-way teleconference: Mahesh, he and I. In the space of fifteen minutes, tickets are arranged for my brother, his family and I to fly to Chennai.

Flying to Chennai hasn't even occurred to me. I guess certain regions of the brain are automatically rewired when you begin to wear the mom hat.

Ruki's wildest dreams have come true. She's been appointed student assistant for the contest play, *Rabbit Hole*. Rehearsals are due to begin today; the day of Amma's passing. It's also the middle of the semester. Classes are in full swing. *She needs to be here. And so, I need to be here.* Girish is scheduled to fly to India on a business trip. The processing in my synapses refuses to travel beyond those boundaries.

So, when I hear Girish say something on the call about Indian currency for *my* trip, my circuits fire all wrong.

'For your trip to Chennai,' he clarifies.

'*My* trip ... but how can I? Ruki's play, her semester has just begun ...' I mumble.

'Sweetheart, you have to go,' he says. 'Everything else can be taken care of.'

'What about Ruki? You're travelling to India on work, you said.'

'Ruki's a bright kid. She can go with me. Missing ten days of school is not the end of the world,' he assures me.

'But—'

'—If you don't go, you'll regret it all your life. I don't want that for you,' he says.

I think about his words, that I'll be dogged by a giant regret all my life. Yes, I have to go. *I want to go.* There's no place I'd rather be than home with Appa and my siblings.

Thirty minutes later, Girish rushes into the living room and holds me tight as I fall apart in his arms. There are no words for this moment. The smell of him, my cheek against his shoulder, and his warmth around me – I draw comfort from it in a way I simply can't from words. Nothing he says now is going to come out right. Nothing anyone says is going to.

My husband is a man of action. He starts to grab clothes from my closet and pack my suitcase, as I wander from living room to bedroom to Ruki's room and back again. A lost soul.

'We have to tell Ruki,' he says, folding a pair of jeans.

I blink. But she's in school, I think. Her life is still well-ordered, one fifty-minute class following another, nothing more challenging to deal with than French verb conjugations and Shakespeare's antiquated language. A part of me doesn't want to disrupt that.

There's no choice. We have to.

I follow Girish down the building stairs and climb into our Honda.

Our neighbour, Marianne, is walking towards the building, hunched against the cold, dwarfed by a thick black winter coat. My eyes take in her greasy hair and austere appearance. She has renounced items that draw attention to the self, like cosmetics and jewellery, in favour of *Plain Jane* piety.

'I think you should tell her,' Girish says.

Marianne has been praying, lighting candles, petitioning the Lord on my behalf, intensifying her efforts when I told her Amma's cancer had spread to the liver. It's strange how I cannot remember a single detail about Amma's deterioration. That part of my memory is a blank slate. What exactly did Maya tell me?

Did she say anything at all? I thought Amma was doing a great job of fighting the cancer and on the road to a full recovery. Why is all this stuff scrambled in my head?

I climb out of the car and walk towards her. 'I just got the news. My mother … passed away,' I say, doing everything I can to hold my tears in.

Marianne shakes her head, stares down at the snow-covered ground, looks up at me again. 'I'm so sorry,' she says, searching my face. And then, as God's insider, adds, 'But I've been getting the message. The Lord told me she would've suffered more if she'd lived.' Her face is a clean sheet of paper, calm in the face of catastrophe.

'I have to go,' I say, at a sudden loss for words. 'My daughter … we have to tell her … she's in school. I'm leaving for India tonight.' It comes out in a jumble.

I take leave. Marianne assures me she will keep us in her prayers.

It's three in the afternoon when we get to school. We approach Student Services where Girish does all the talking. I'm scared to open my mouth, not trusting the sounds that might spill out. So I contain myself, hold in my deep despair. Student Services pages Ruki. It's surreal, listening to the announcement boom, bounce, echo through the hallways: 'Rukmeeni Girsh, please come to the main office … Rukmeeni Girsh to the main office …'

I stand there, desperate to flee. Where am I going to find the words to tell my daughter that the grandma she adores is no longer alive? I, the family wordsmith, have suddenly lost the power to craft one sensitive sentence.

Within moments, Ruki is walking towards us, her steps quickening, with an expression of: 'Surely you guys remember I have rehearsal' crowding her face. I want to be the good mother, strong in the midst of a crisis, but I can't find my voice. Girish takes over, rescues the situation.

Gently, he places his hands on her shoulders, looks into her eyes and utters the dreadful words. 'Ruki, Paati ... passed away.'

'What!?'

Shades of shock, awe and bewilderment flicker across her small, innocent face as she struggles with the awful truth.

'Mamma's leaving for Chennai tonight. Go, get your backpack. We need to go home, organize everything, and get her on a plane.'

Ruki is like her dad in most respects, a fact I'm especially thankful for right this minute. She turns around and marches off, all business now. I can tell she's very aware of her surroundings and has opted for an emotional hiatus for the time being.

Moments later as we're driving home, she stares out the window, tears streaming down her face. I rub her back, hot tears sliding down my cheeks.

2

I'M IN THE KITCHEN STEAMING RICE DUMPLINGS FOR dinner. For brief snatches of time, my mind is engaged and distracted. Then a fresh wave of grief knocks me over, and I dissolve into tears.

The dumplings are about done when my brother walks in the front door, followed by his wife and three-year-old son. It is half-past five in the evening.

I cry in his arms; he, more than anyone else, knows what a huge loss this is. He and I have shared a life with this beloved woman we're mourning. The grief is woven into our membranes, sewn into our nerve endings. She gave us life; in her death, the spirit goes out of us.

An hour later, Girish drives us to O'Hare. As soon as we get to the airport, I call Maya. Hang in there, we'll be there real soon, I offer, minimizing a twenty-two-hour transatlantic journey. My mind is spinning as we pick up boarding passes and go through security check. *Where is Amma's* – my mind stumbles here – *body*? My brain cannot fathom the vocabulary. It was her body that gave me life. And now, she's just a 'body with no life!' All I know at this time is that her body will be embalmed in readiness for our arrival.

I wonder how Appa is coping. Who broke the news to him? What words did they use?

As I walk into the aircraft, a flight attendant parrots his pet phrase: 'Have a pleasant flight.'

I eyeball him. 'That's a little difficult. I just lost my mother and I'm flying to India for her last rites.' He flushes, averts his eyes, and mumbles an apology. I know it's not his fault; he's just doing his job.

But I'm feeling prickly.

Through all the despair, a single thought warms me. I'm grateful to be travelling with my brother. I shudder as the alternative hits me. Under different circumstances, I might've been making this sad, long journey alone.

If you've been in a car rushing to rescue a loved one in an emergency, you know the feeling. You stare out of the window, watch the landscape whiz by, and yell at whoever is driving you to hit the gas pedal, encourage him to break a few speed barriers. There are things you can seemingly control.

I'm strapped in an airplane seat, nothing but a thick bank of clouds outside my window. I feel trapped. There's not a thing I can do to speed anything along except mentally chant: hurry, hurry, hurry!

3

$\mathcal{I}$T IS A TWENTY-TWO-HOUR JOURNEY: CHICAGO–
FRANKFURT–MUMBAI, followed by a Mumbai–Chennai
domestic transfer. Given that it's the end of January, our
international flight is virtually empty: ample room to stretch out
on an entire three-seater row. Mahesh has wandered off to find
another empty row. In the midst of this ocean of sorrow, we still
need to find our own private islands of solitude.

A vacant flight also saves me some embarrassment: my tear
ducts are on overdrive. I try to lose myself in a book, but after re-
reading the same two lines for over an hour, I give up. What keeps
me afloat is my journal. I pour my grief into it; it soaks everything
up, uncomplaining, non-judgmental.

My mental screen is awash with images of Amma: I see her
folding laundry, perched in front of the television and riveted by
the twists and turns in the lives of her favourite soap characters;
teasing Appa; bathing the brass deities that grace her altar; picking
out jewellery to match her silk saris, and even head scarves post-
chemo. These are just a handful of images from the millions in my
memory bank.

They are all I have now.

I sneak a glance at my brother who is slumped in a seat across
the aisle. His eyes are closed, his lips move in a silent chant. We
haven't talked much; we don't know what to say. But when we do,
we worry aloud about Appa. My brother's wife is totally occupied
with their toddler's unceasing demands. It occurs to me that I'm
a stranger to this little boy, my nephew. The extended family has
been cordoned off from him, an innocent child caught in the
crossfire.

I never imagined my world without Amma. Being the oldest, I have travelled many tough roads with her – what will I do without her? I'm bereft. I've just lost the map and must navigate solo through uncharted territory.

It is the end of an era. Our family, as I have always known it, is now changed forever.

Amma, I miss you with every breath I take. Talk to me; tell me how to go on. I don't know how to do this … alone.

It is morning when we disembark in Mumbai. Strangely, once we're in India I feel physically closer to Amma. Amma is in India; so am I now.

Waiting for immigration formalities, I spot an old friend of mine. She's standing at a chaat counter, munching bhel puri. She used to lead our Chennai Writers' group, before moving to Mumbai when her husband's company transferred him. It's been almost five years since we lost touch. Glimpsing her face now brings back a rush of memories of simpler, happier times, when one of life's major preoccupations was playing with prose, tweaking a turn of phrase.

It takes me about three seconds to decide. I have no wish to renew ties in this context. I'm loath to open my mouth and speak the dreadful words: why I'm here and what I'm doing. I turn away, hide behind a magazine, dart glances her way to make sure my cover is not blown until she disappears into the crowds.

The Mumbai–Chennai domestic transfer is a nightmare. We go through security, load everything in a coach, clamber aboard and endure a sweaty, smelly, shoulder-to-shoulder ride to the terminal.

4

In the Indian tradition, a body is sent to the morgue only if immediate family members need to fly across several time zones. Whether it is at the hospital or the morgue, the body is brought home, and makes the final journey for cremation from there.

Amma is waiting for us.

As a result, the final leg of the journey tests every last ounce of my patience. I don't have the equanimity for a 90-minute domestic flight plus all the attendant formalities. All I want is to be teleported home, to Maya, Guru, Vidu and Appa.

It is half-past ten in the morning on the 29 January, thirty-six hours after Amma's passing. We're finally in Chennai. The cool breeze outside the airport makes me shiver. Girish's local office has sent a van to meet us.

We cruise past buildings and landmarks I've navigated a thousand times, and everything is the same, yet everything looks different. As if draped over it all is a terrible pall of gloom. India has always been a veritable feast for the senses, but now the landscape is an endless sadness of dull, leaden grey.

As we drive closer to Amma's neighbourhood, a pang pierces me. A visceral pain.

There's the shop Amma bought tulsi leaves, roses and marigolds from, on festival days. That's the hosiery shop she frequented for her nightgowns. Amma's tailor, snack shop, plumber …

All of a sudden it snags my eye. An ambulance with a bright red cross emblazoned on the back, driving just ahead of our van. Inside the back window of the vehicle, I spot a glass coffin. The ambulance turns left and so do we; it makes a right and we're right behind; it makes a U-turn at the next intersection and we do the same.

Panic flutters in my belly.

Amma's in there.

My heart speeds up; my mouth is sandpaper-dry. I can't swallow.

Everything is moving towards that moment when I must view my mother's lifeless body. The very thought repels. I chase it away.

As we turn the last corner towards Seashore Apartments, the ambulance pulls into the building's parking lot. I'm still struggling to process the reality that the vehicle ahead of us has a body in it – Amma's body.

Friends and family crowd the driveway. Relatives, neighbours, random strangers, faces and names register for a millisecond, then fade away. The three of us, my nephew on my sister-in-law's hip, walk into the courtyard, all eyes swivelling in our direction.

I see Maya and Vidu, and rush into my sisters' arms. Vidu, I know, flew in from Bahrain this morning. We hold each other and cry as survivors do, unmindful of the onlookers.

Maya quickly wipes her eyes, draws us all into a huddle. 'There's something you need to know.' Her somber tone alerts me.

What can you possibly say that could devastate me any more?

As we listen, Maya says, 'Appa suffered a seizure yesterday. He's in hospital.'

Ever since the road accident – a couple of bikers knocked Appa off his scooter and sped away – fourteen years ago and a brain injury, Appa has been seizure-prone. He is on powerful anti-epilepsy medications, but Amma's passing is, I imagine, a nine-point-something on his personal Richter scale.

My jaw clenches as fresh pain washes over me. *How much more does he – or any of us – need to take?*

Maya explains, 'A team of doctors is bringing him home for Amma's last rites. And he'll be taken back to the hospital. We need to stay, well, at least pretend to stay calm for as long as he's here. If we get overly emotional, he's going to be even more devastated. And we can't let that happen.'

We walk indoors, past the assortment of footwear scattered by the sides of the front door. The living room is crowded with people: uncles, aunts, cousins, sisters-in-law, brothers-in-law, Amma's cousins and their spouses. It is a sea of grief-stricken expressions. They move towards me, weighed down by sadness, hold me, stroke my hair, whisper clichés and walk away.

I step into Maya's bedroom. Paati, my beloved grandmother, ninety-one and bereaved. Something sharp and jagged stabs my chest as my eyes settle on her, register the indescribable sadness that pools in her eyes. She looks like someone who's lost everything in life, her lips quivering with the effort to contain the unspeakable sorrow.

'She left us all … went away.' Paati spreads her palms out in a helpless gesture, triggering fresh tears in me.

Someone bustles in. 'Hurry up, have a bath. The priest says it's getting late.'

All of us need to bathe, be purified if you will, before the last rites commence. I need clothes and I can't remember if I brought my bags in, or where they are.

'Here,' someone wheels my orange suitcase into the room.

Maya rushes in for a moment, hands me one of Amma's silk saris. I suffer a moment of panic. I can't remember if I packed a sari blouse.

My little sister reads my expression. 'You can wear mine,' she says and leaves the room, returning moments later with a matching blouse.

There are people everywhere, in every room. Finding a tiny wedge of space in the overcrowded bedroom, I open my suitcase and extract my clothes. With what looks like ten people monitoring my every move, I step into the bathroom, shut the door, and breathe in a moment of private peace. My arms are full of clothes – except for the sari which must be worn in the room, yards and yards of silk puddling on the floor.

I take the fastest bath of my life, drape the sari, and slip bangles onto my wrist, hearing Amma's voice in my head: *You don't perform a ritual with bare wrists.*

The constant din inside my head is louder than all the noise outside. It is the soundtrack of grief – discordant, mournful keening and wailing.

I glance at Vidu, feel a pang. Her situation is unenviable. As if Amma's loss weren't enough to handle, life is tugging her in other directions as well. Her husband suffered a massive heart attack three weeks before Amma passed away. He is in fragile health, recuperating at home after bypass surgery. His dressings need to be changed regularly, medicines monitored carefully, and a heart-healthy diet followed to a T. Throw their five-year-old son into the mix, and Vidu almost didn't make it to Chennai. It was her husband who convinced her to go. She's due to fly back to Bahrain in forty-eight hours.

Even in the horrific aftermath of a grievous loss, we must consider our blessings.

Now that I'm 'purified', I must do what I've been dreading: look at Amma's still, lifeless body. Someone who laughed with her entire being and was just a beautiful incandescent spirit, it's impossible to imagine her essence stilled.

I dawdle, rearrange a sari pleat, and tuck the *pallu* in.

By now, the glass coffin must be in the middle of the room for people to pay their last respects.

I step out of the room having done everything possible to delay, avoid and push away the moment. My feet feel like blocks of concrete. The two-foot walk to the coffin is suddenly a mile long. Every step I take empties my lungs, like the life force is ebbing away from me. Nothing has prepared me for this moment.

I double over when I reach her. The mother who gave me life is now a lifeless being trapped inside a glass coffin. My fingers claw at the glass like I'm clinging to the edge of a cliff. Her face is bloated, her stomach distended, her skin thick and bluish-grey. Her ears and nostrils are stuffed with cotton balls.

This is not Amma. This is not the Amma I know and love. This is not what she looks like.

I flinch, turn away and fall into Aunt Chandra's waiting arms.

My aunt holds me, strokes my hair, shushes me like she used to when I was a kindergartner. History repeats itself. She'd had to literally peel me off her when I bawled to go inside the school building.

This time, though, my body is not stiff or arching in anger. This is loose-limbed grief. This is me crumbling into pieces and wondering if I'll ever be whole again. The pain, a twisting tunnel of darkness, takes up all the room inside me.

I turn, grab at the coffin again. My fingers leave ugly smears on the glass. I hear the moans – 'Amma … Amma …' – coming from a dark space inside me. It's almost easy to believe that my calling out in this anguished voice is sure to awaken her, have her sit up and ask, 'When did you arrive?'

In the deepest part of my being I know this is wishful thinking. She's never coming back. The world has changed forever.

5

$\mathcal{I}$T IS TIME TO BATHE AND DRESS AMMA'S COLD, LIFELESS form. It is for Vidu, Maya and I to do this. Amma's body is now out of the glass coffin, and lying on the cool mosaic floor in the centre of the living room.

Glancing at her a second time, I notice it. A shock ripples through me. Amma's head is uncovered. No one remembered to drape the scarf. Instinctively, I want to rush over and cover her head with one of her bright scarves. For eight months, she hid her bald-baby look from the rest of the world. By the time our transatlantic flight arrived in Chennai, she's been exposed. There's one thing I know for sure: Amma was so proud of her hair she would've died before letting anyone see her that way.

A married woman's last journey is always in an elegant silk sari.

But my eyes linger over her peach nightie now, the last earthly garment she wore in the world of the living. Next, I take in her red plastic bangles, one on each wrist. My eyes come to rest on the middle toe of her left foot. It seems broken, the very sight makes my insides curl, scream.

A bearded priest stands beside Amma's body. He smells of holy ash and chants in a singsong voice. Suddenly, he stops chanting and starts to talk. I snap out of my reverie. He glances at his wristwatch, checks for the auspicious moment, pronounces, 'It's time to start,' then barks out orders. The three of us follow his step-by-step instructions.

The first order of business is the symbolic last bath. We each fill a shining brass pot to the brim with holy water. The priest tells me to splash the water all over Amma's body, using the fingers of my right hand to guide its trajectory. As Amma's eldest daughter I go first, followed by Vidu, and then Maya. A panicked bird beats its wings inside my chest. As I splash the water, it whooshes out of the pot and hits her face and nostrils, drenches her nightie.

She just lies there, unresisting.

I flinch.

This, if nothing else, brings home the truth with a brutal finality.

Amma's gone.

She's not in there any more. Not in the curve of the shoulder I've known; not in the crook of the elbow I held so often; not in the soft, fleshy arms I loved to stroke. It is a moment of pure terror, a moment when my insides feel gutted.

Maya, Vidu and I go through the motions, performing a series of tasks that at once wrench the heart and cause us to fumble and stumble in painful ignorance.

You can't have a dress rehearsal for death.

Someone has picked out a sari for Amma to wear: a rich mango-yellow silk with a magenta border, colours of celebration. In the Hindu tradition, dying before one's husband is the highest honour a married woman aspires to. To leave her earthly abode first, to die a *sumangali* is a guarantee of salvation. Amma gave all of herself – mind, body and soul – to the one man she made a commitment to, honouring every word of her sacred wedding vows till her last breath. Her greatest reward comes in death. She is a true sumangali. Yet, knowing Amma, I'm absolutely certain she'd have turned the offer down if she'd had a choice in the matter. Escaping to another realm while Appa struggles here all alone in his earthly avatar would be unthinkable for her.

I ponder the irony, rubbing fresh turmeric paste on her cheeks, forehead and feet, my streaming eyes clouding my vision. Her body is ice-cold. I apply a dot of bright red kumkum powder on the wet turmeric; fix a red bindi in the centre of her forehead; smudge more kumkum on her non-existent hair parting. Then I place flowers – jasmine and marigolds – at the top of her head, and a makeshift *thaali*, the sacred chain married women wear, around her neck. It is a simple silk thread with a root of turmeric, a symbolic thaali. The gold chain she wore, the real thaali, came off Maya tells me, as soon as she was pronounced dead at the hospital. It lies safely ensconced in Amma's jewellery box now.

We tuck swirls of the silk sari around her. I slip my handwritten ten-page letter into the sari folds. I'd started writing it about ten days before she passed away, certain that Girish who was embarking on his India business trip would hand-deliver it to Amma.

She never got to read the letter.

⟨⟨∙⟩∙⟨⟩⟩

'The hospital van is here,' someone shouts, and we all prepare for Appa's arrival.

6

I WIPE MY EYES AND COMPOSE MY FEATURES, WONDERING what 'acceptable' grief looks like.

When I look up, Appa's frail frame fills the doorway, a hospital attendant positioned on either side of him.

Stooped over his walker, Appa looks like a man who's lost his way in the world. His eyes are vacant, a day-old stubble deepening the shadows of grief.

A well of sympathy rushes up from deep within me. For a moment, I set aside my pain, my loss and reflect upon what Amma's passing is doing to this man. It is the abrupt and unexpected ending of a long and complicated relationship that traversed hills and vales over forty-seven long years.

Someone has positioned a chair beside Amma's body. Slowly, Appa lowers himself into it. He looks at Amma, tears spilling from his eyes. The four of us – Maya, Mahesh, Vidu and I – circle him, almost protectively, stroke his back. The language of touch comes to one's aid where words fail.

He starts talking to Amma.

'What will I do without you … how could you leave me here and go away?'

While Amma was alive, Appa rarely paused to contemplate if she had the physical time or mental space to listen. It was a tacit agreement: when he spoke, she listened. And she did, her dark eyes dancing with energy, head cocked to the side, a half-smile on her lips.

Now, for the first time, she doesn't respond in the way he knows or understands. I look away, heartsick, trying to shut out his words. Pain skewers me as I witness my father carry on a one-sided conversation with my deceased mother. The four of us make some pathetic attempts at consoling him.

You still have us. We're with you. You'll never be alone. Amma would want you to be happy. Parroting empty words, we soon run out of confusing clichés. Clearly, it's not enough. Nothing is. Nothing will ever be enough to fill this huge chasm, the empty void in his heart, his world.

In that instant, I become conscious of our changed circle. Amma was the Ramachandran family sun, the rest of us orbiting her for warmth, direction and counsel. Now, friends and family are watching us: four grown children trying, and hopelessly failing to console their bereaved father.

Ten minutes later, the medical attendants gesture to us. Can we take him back, their eyes ask. It's a signal that Appa is on emotional overload and needs a break. We consult each other and give them our consent. There's nothing more to do.

Watching Appa walk away with a couple of white-coated attendants, feels like sending your baby away with strangers.

The priest pronounces the auspicious moment for the last journey to begin.

Pall-bearers take their positions.

They pick up Amma's body and place it on a bamboo bier. They hoist the bier and carry her out of the house and into the front yard. More rituals follow. We circle the bier seven times, sprinkle rice grains on her mouth, and holy water over her body one last time. Amma has just been fed her last meal before her soul's journey begins.

People are crowding in for one last look, many of them dabbing their eyes: cleaning maids from the apartments, drivers, neighbours, the flower-seller, the sweeper. The woman who irons clothes for a living walks up, and tearfully touches Amma's feet. It is a gesture of taking the blessing of the departed, now believed to be one among the gods. Curiosity-mongers peek through windows from homes on the other floors, all eager for a piece of the spectacle – The Other's Grief.

Although this is certainly not the image of Amma I wish to carry in my head, I can't stop staring at her. Soon the physical reality of her will be lost to me forever. If it isn't already. I can barely breathe, as realization dawns that I will never again see her smile, hold her or smell the strong post-shower whiff of turmeric cream wafting from her.

The pall-bearers lift the bier, load it in the back of the ambulance, and shut the door. I want to climb inside, hold on tight and never let go. But the elders hold me back. The crematorium is a place where only dead women are allowed. It's strictly off-limits for living, breathing women.

What about living men? Why do they get to go? I'm tempted to fight back as Mahesh and my uncle get into the vehicle. The driver turns the key in the ignition. The vehicle rolls out of the parking lot and turns the corner. Amma takes her last earthly ride – to the crematorium – with her brother, and her son who will immerse her ashes in the ocean and ensure her salvation.

7

*I*T'S TIME FOR A SECOND ROUND OF PURIFICATION BATHS. Wash away the death. *How can I,* my mind screams. Can you catch death, I wonder. Amma's death is a part of me, like a second skin I'll wear for the rest of my life.

After baths, we start to purify the house, sloshing bucketfuls of water on the mosaic floor where Amma's body lay just minutes ago, then sweep the water out of the house with a coconut-reed broom.

Thankfully, the house has emptied; people have gone back to their regular homes and lives. Grief is private. But in our culture, mourning is public.

I want to draw into my cocoon of sorrow and live there. The only people I can tolerate at this time are my siblings, the three people who share the same raw, gutted-out pain.

We sit on the floor, the four of us, and start to talk. As far back as I can recall, it's what we know how to do, what we've done, when times were tough. No matter if it was Appa's drunken binge or a violent epileptic fit, we've turned to words to help stitch together the frayed bits of ourselves. Words have always been salve to our deepest wounds.

There's so much that Mahesh, Vidu and I don't know about Amma's last hours. My mind and heart and body did not ever want to believe, to accept, that this is how it would all end. Even when there is forewarning, as in a cancer diagnosis, the end feels all too sudden.

Maya was sole witness to the last few scenes of Amma's horrific descent. Now it is her job to recount the details as we train our expectant eyes on her.

She looks at us, her eyes darting from one to the other. I sense the enormity of the task ahead of her. Where do I begin, her face seems to ask. Bit by bit, breath by breath, she begins to piece it together for us.

'She started to go downhill on Pongal day,' Maya starts.

The harvest festival on 14 January was one of Amma's favourite celebrations, the day we were treated to chakkara pongal – cashew-studded rice pudding sweetened with jaggery and flavoured with ghee.

'She was up early, bathed and doing puja. She insisted on bathing all the deities and making the chakkara pongal. By the time lunch was over, I could see she was exhausted, struggling to move.' Maya pauses in the narrative, takes a breath. 'It was the beginning of the end,' she whispers.

I feel a moment of irrational anger at all those deities who let her down. *This is what she got for washing you and feeding you her divine pongal!*

From Pongal day, Amma took to lying in bed for long periods of time. Her appetite had all but vanished; the pain on her right side began to worsen. It became so unbearable it tested even her genial, uncomplaining self.

'I feel useless,' 'I'm not interested in anything,' 'I can't do anything,' became her oft-repeated phrases.

On the morning of 21 January, Amma had doubled over in excruciating pain. Maya made an emergency call to the oncologist who ordered them to rush her to the hospital. Three hours of waiting and a series of tests, including an ultrasound of the abdomen, had revealed the worst.

There were multiple lesions in her liver.

We brought Amma home after seeking permission from the doctor. By this time, Amma couldn't eat a morsel without clutching her stomach and crying out in pain. She could barely hobble from her bed to the front door, a distance of twelve feet. The cancer had metastasized to her lungs and liver; her entire body yellowed with the sickly pallor of jaundice. Days and nights were spent in throes of pain. Her ribcage, back and sides hurt constantly.

The oncologist had only one suggestion: another regimen of chemotherapy. Amma was so debilitated by now that even a ride to the hospital seemed a huge undertaking.

This one memory is intact: Maya's phone call and how we, as a family, took that painful decision. All her life, Amma had been happy to hand over the reins of decision-making in all matters to Appa. After Appa's accident, the mantle passed to the four of us.

No more chemo, we decided. Amma simply didn't have the energy to endure the long, traffic-choked ride to the hospital, the unending wait for a bed, the IV drip and the long ride back home.

Dr R did the next best thing. He started her on pain medication. Most of the time she was barely able to tell the difference between night and day; she was so woozy she refused food and even stopped going to the bathroom.

This must have been a serious red flag moment for Maya.

Even through the earlier chemo regimens, Amma had never given up. She kept going. She fussed over Appa, made his coffee, served him breakfast, mashed his foods and supervised his medicines.

That, by the third week of January, she lay in a bed right next to him, completely unaware of his needs, must have been very telling.

―――――――<⸱⸱●⸱●⸱>―――――――

All I remember is the escalating panic and urgency in our e-mail exchanges of those two weeks. At some point the e-mailing had stopped; we'd simply taken to calling each other, and particularly Maya who was in the eye of the storm. We needed more than cold, blank words on a computer screen; we needed the reassuring, hopeful rhythms and cadences in each other's voices.

But now, something strange happens. As Maya recollects the terrible ordeal of those weeks – how Amma's body was giving up, one organ at a time – my brain responds to it like brand new information.

'Did you really tell me that?' I ask her, disbelief creeping into my voice.

She gives me a peculiar look. 'Everything,' she says.

'Really!?' I repeat. 'I don't remember a thing.' As her narrative unfolds, I say it again and again, every third sentence. It's almost as if those phone calls never happened. My mental files come up completely blank. This is the nature of false hope. That same hope lies shattered now, shards of glass we're crunching over.

Clearly, my brain was in shut-down mode, stalling any information that signalled Amma's possible end. What I do remember is a tenacious, fighting hope, a clinging and cleaving to a faith that my God would, somehow, work a miracle and turn it around for Amma, and all of us.

Almost a year later, the realization will dawn on me. I will continue to mourn Amma in a way that baffles my siblings who do a much better job of acceptance, and coming to peace. It was hope that betrayed me, led me down the garden path with its silky seductive lure. I actually followed hope to a place where I believed the best outcome was not only possible, but a given. My husband will look at me, his face full of incredulity: 'I knew when the cancer spread to her liver ... that it was a matter of time.' His eyes say: *Don't tell me you didn't know that. Really!?* If truth be told, I didn't. Call it denial, call it blind faith, call it an unwillingness to let go, call it what you will.

Over the next days, I am obsessive. I pound Maya with questions. What did Amma say on her last day? Did she talk to Appa? Did she know it was her time? How did she look? Did she ask about me? Or Vidu? Or Mahesh? How long did she sleep? Were there moments when she had some relief from pain? The questions will grow in number over the following days. Not having been a part of Amma's world in her last few days I will try to experience it vicariously, devouring any scrap of information Maya can give me.

'She was waiting to say goodbye to Paati,' Maya says.

My uncle, aunt and Paati had visited just minutes before the end. Considerably weak by then, Amma had hobbled to the living room, leaning heavily on Maya. Sinking into a chair, she'd drifted on and off in a drowsy, drug-induced haze, offering monosyllabic responses to their questions. Paati was working hard to bolster Amma's confidence, telling her that she'd offered special prayers to a deity who was renowned for his healing powers. To which Amma had come up with a complete sentence. 'Only God can save me now.' He had, on His terms.

Maya had complained to my aunt that Amma had adamantly refused food all day. Aunt had coaxed and cajoled her, successfully got her to eat an entire banana. That was Amma's last supper.

It had taken my uncle forty-five minutes in thick traffic to drive home. As he entered their third-floor apartment, my aunt and Paati following, the landline was ringing off the hook. It was Maya choking out the dreaded words.

Amma was gone.

'So, tell me, what happened after they left,' I say. 'Was she still sitting here in the living room?'

'No, she got really tired even before they left. Said she wanted to go lie down,' Maya explains. 'By the time everyone left, it was late and I had to get Appa's dinner ready. I was in the kitchen when I heard her call my name. Her voice was really feeble. I ran to the bedroom. She was moaning, and restless. The nurse was rubbing her feet. Amma's feet are too cold, she kept saying. I started to rub too.

'All of a sudden, Amma's eyes were rolling back. Then I hear the nurse shout to me, "We need to rush her to the hospital." Amma's back was arching and she looked really strange. Guru had gone to the pharmacy with a new prescription, so I ran to the front door and started to shout for help. Then I dialed Dr V (Appa's physiotherapist, who was more like a member of the family). Neighbours rushed in. Meantime, Guru also showed up. I banged on auntie's door, told her to keep an eye on Appa.'

Maya's voice trembles. She dabs at her eyes. 'The guys picked her up and carried her to the back seat of the car. Her head was resting on the nurse's lap. I've never seen Guru drive the way he did that night ...'

The tears don't stop. She pauses to wipe them. 'She didn't make it to the hospital. The nurse told me Amma took her last breaths right outside the temple. She'd have been happy about that.' An ironic laugh follows.

Sorrow swells in my throat. I swallow around it. I don't want to hear any more. I want to hear every last, gristly detail.

An insatiable hunger gnaws inside me. It's like feeding a monster with a bottomless stomach, this need to recycle painful images. It's an endless loop regurgitated by my imagination, of Amma's words and actions in the last two weeks of her life, a time I've missed forever.

At this point, someone I don't recognize interrupts Maya's story-telling. He walks through the front door, deposits a few stainless steel containers of food on the table. A relative I don't know? A neighbour? A caterer?

Aunt had cautioned us before she left. Don't light the stove, you're not allowed to cook anything for the next three days. We'll bring you your meals.

It's confusing, all these dos and don'ts, but in our culture, 'why' is not a welcome word. The unasked whys rattle in my head: why aren't we supposed to light the stove? Why aren't women allowed inside a crematorium? Why did we feed Amma rice grains when she was long gone?

But I swallow them all. When elders instruct, you simply follow. Never question.

In any case, food is the last thing on my mind.

Food, however, was Amma's passion. The prospect of trying a

new recipe or a novel culinary tip had never failed to produce a rush of adrenaline. She loved nothing more than to cook elaborate meals and serve her creations to friends, neighbours and family. She'd watch people's mouths close around the food, and eagerly await feedback. I always wondered how feeding a family of six for forty-some years hadn't blunted her culinary ardour.

Now there's a dull, flat taste in my mouth, a revolting response to those gigantic containers of food.

'You must eat, even if it's a little. Keep your strength up,' a friend advises.

We oblige and pick at the food. It's easier than trying to argue or explain how appetite is the first thing a hole in the soul kills.

8

$\mathcal{I}$'M SLEEP-DEPRIVED, SLEEP-STARVED – AN INSOMNIAC. Topsy-turvy time zones and fresh grief are a toxic combination.

I sit in the living room. It has been stripped of its familiar furniture format. Everything was moved, shifted earlier in the day to make room for the religious rituals and the mourners in attendance. Now the room is empty, empty, empty – the word rattles inside my head.

There is ample room for grief here. Greedily, it crowds into cobwebby corners and hangs, a stark eerie silence choking the life-breath out of the house. This house without Amma is a body without a soul; a vacant brick-and-mortar structure, a shell, lifeless.

I have offered to stay the night with Appa in the hospital room. Everything inside me screams at having to leave the safe nest where my brother and sisters are; yet, a part of me cannot abandon Appa to a night all by himself on a hard metal cot in a sad hospital room, paint peeling off the walls.

I leave home at six in the evening. Stepping outside, I feel threatened; everything makes me tremble. The world has suddenly become an unsafe place. Neighbours stop and stare, their eyes sad and sympathetic, their heads tilted just so, their faces and voices dripping with pity. Poor motherless you, they are thinking. I just know it.

Appa is sleeping when I let myself into his room. His body is pumped with a lot of powerful medicines. I settle down on the hard cot provided for the family attendant, its rigid ribs poking through the thin mattress. I lie down and close my eyes, knowing better than to blame my upcoming sleepless night on a hospital mattress.

During the night, every time Appa stirs, I'm alert. Just when I've managed to nod off, I hear creaking and groaning. My eyes snap open. Appa is sitting up in bed. I need to go to the bathroom, he says. I support him, get him off the bed and into the bathroom, and turn on the light. Once he's safely back in bed I close my eyes, but it's difficult to slip behind the slinky veil of sleep. Appa tosses in bed all night, his legs moving restlessly, trying to find a comfortable position.

After what seems like an endless night, the thin light of an early dawn leaks through the grimy windows of the room. I stay in bed, entertaining fantasies that sleep will claim me, grant me the gift of oblivion for a couple of hours.

And then, without a warning, it starts: the lonely lament.

Appa is staring at the ceiling, his sad eyes fixed on a distant spot as he starts talking to Amma. Slowly, I sit up straight. He lets loose a wild stream of unintelligible sorrow. It pours out of him, a long, winding river of melancholy.

'Why did you leave me … I'm all alone now … where have you gone to … I don't want to go home now … what is left there … only the four empty walls of our room … I can't see you … how will I go on …'

On and on, the lament continues. This naked display of emotion shocks and numbs me at the same time. When I've managed to staunch the flow of my tears, I step up to his bed and take his cold, clammy hand in mine. 'Appa … we're all here for you … me, Vidu, Mahesh and Maya. We'll take care of you. You'll never be alone, I promise.'

Easy words to speak; difficult actions to commit to.

To my ears they sound like an equally unintelligible stream of words, a senseless jumble of syllables that contain no comfort. Even as the words leave my lips, I feel their emptiness. How can we ever be enough? Losing a wife is hard enough; losing a wife like Amma is monumental. She's irreplaceable, one of a kind. What are we going to do without her?

A wellspring of sadness gushes up from deep within. I drop his hand and flee the room, unable to stand in the space of Appa's wailing sorrow. I sit on the bench in the narrow corridor and cry my eyes out, grateful for the din of the morning – honking buses and autorickshaws, vegetable and fruit vendors, people on the roads – that drowns out my noisy sobs.

A nurse finds me. 'Don't worry. Your father's doing well. He should be discharged later today,' she consoles, completely missing the point.

Like some desperate, needy creature I hasten to fill her in on the tragic turn of events in my life. 'Amma looked after him with such devotion. Now he's like a child who's lost his mother, more than a husband who's lost his wife. This is going to be so difficult. I don't know if he's ever going to be okay.'

She holds my hand, listens attentively, nods and clucks in sympathy. Then she offers to bring me some tea. While she's gone, I pull out my cell phone and call home. Mahesh answers on the second ring. 'I can't do this ... it's so difficult to see him so lost, so sad,' I explain what just happened in the room.

'You need a break. Let me get something to eat and I'll be over. You need to come home and rest,' he says, his voice a warm breeze.

As I sip the tea the nurse hands me, I take in the landscape. The morning air is tinged with pungent fumes spewing from the tailpipes of city buses roaring down the street. The leaves on the trees are a depressing green-grey, layered with a thick coating of dust. A sweeper swishes her broom across the street, raising huge clouds of dust. A few morning walkers soldier on, firmly focused on the business of shedding pounds. How can people get on buses and take morning walks and sweep roads and open their flower shops as if life were normal? Amma just died. Nothing about this life feels normal any more. And yet, life goes on. It's business as usual for the rest of the world. I experience an intense sense of alienation, a feeling of utter separateness, detached from everybody and everything, floating in ether, a desolate spirit.

Guilty at having abandoned Appa, I crack open the door to his room and peer in. The mighty monster, my father's grief, terrifies me. I don't want to face it. I can barely deal with my own. I hand Appa a glass of hot tea as compensation for my unexplained absence. In the slow, deliberate sipping of it and the moments of silence we find a tiny measure of peace.

When Mahesh arrives, I greet him like a lost survivor who's finally caught sight of the rescue squad. 'I'll stay on till evening and wait for the doctor. Let's see what he has to say. I wonder how long they'll keep Appa here,' Mahesh says.

My feeling of relief is distinctly guilt-edged as I grab my overnighter and leave the room feeling like I've failed my father.

9

I GET HOME AND COLLAPSE INTO BED UTTERLY EXHAUSTED, every limb wrung out with the weight of emotion my body is struggling to contain.

When I wake up, dusky twilight is draping the sky in velvety violet. Still groggy, I stumble into the living room squinting against the milky-white glare of the tube light.

Appa is sitting on the divan, a confused look on his face. He reminds me of a broken bird on the sidewalk, its future uncertain.

'They said he's stable and discharged him,' Mahesh responds to my mystified look. 'We have to monitor his medicines, though – especially his epilepsy pills.'

'Oh!' My brain feels cloudy.

Maya is standing by the telephone, glancing at a prescription. She's about to call the pharmacy.

All this time, a part of me was relieved not to have Appa at home. As long as he was cloistered in a hospital room, someone else was responsible for his well-being. All I had to do was hang around the fringes and offer the bare minimum. Now, I'm back to feeling that I, as the eldest sibling, have to assume the role of parent to my father who finds himself suddenly orphaned by Amma's passing.

I feel a kick in the gut as the question steamrolls me. *What's it going to do to him to walk into the bedroom he shared with Amma, to stare at the now-empty place in the bed beside his own?*

It's enough to bring on a panic attack. I want to flee. I don't want to witness his fresh sorrow, to watch him crumple like a child whose world has, without warning, irrevocably changed.

None of this happens.

'I'll sleep here,' Appa says, patting the divan, declaring his decision with calm clarity.

'Sure,' 'Okay,' 'Fine,' three relief-filled voices respond in chorus.

Over the next few minutes, we figure out the logistics of bed linen and divvying up seven adults and a toddler between two bedrooms and a living room.

I offer to spread a mattress on the living room floor, sleep right beside the divan.

My eyes alight on the small oil lamp flickering in a corner of the room. Beside it is a container of sesame oil. Maya recaps the priest's instructions. Feed the lamp with oil; it must continue to burn for three days and three nights. Another symbolic ritual, the why and how of it lost to me. But the implication is clear. As the one who's going to sleep here, it is my responsibility to keep checking oil levels through the night and top it off.

Appa can't be left alone; nor can the lamp.

Waking up in the living room in middle of the night, Appa is very confused about the geography of the house. A couple of times he heads off in the direction of the front door, thinking it is the bathroom. I escort him to the bathroom three times.

Needless to say, between replenishing the oil level and making sure Appa's not stumbling through the dark to get to the bathroom, I don't get much sleep.

He can barely navigate to the bathroom. How will he navigate through life without Amma by his side?

When my limbs finally relax into sleep-surrender, the phone rings, the doorbell rings, the neighbours, after their eight hours of sweet slumber, are decidedly garrulous.

10

WAKING UP TO APPA'S MOURNFUL LAMENT CRUSHED ME; walking into Amma's kitchen knowing I'll never find her here again is heartbreaking.

The kitchen was Amma's abode, her favourite part of every house we've lived in. This is the space where she created the mouth-watering meals that nourished us, but more importantly, kept us comforted and connected as a family that always ate together.

Just six months ago – during my June visit – I'd woken up here to the rich aroma of milk boiling on the stove. Soon, the pick-me-up smell of fresh coffee would float in on the morning air. I'd hear her chanting in the kitchen, Sanskrit shlokas she'd grown up with.

I picture her in front of the altar, bowed in reverence before her gods, smoke from the sandalwood incense curling towards me.

I ache for the intonation in her voice chanting *Gajananam*, drawing out the second syllable as she lit the lamp. Then she'd pad past me, her house slippers slapping towards the phone and call the store with her usual list of grocery items. It was a family joke that if she didn't call them first thing in the morning, the store's daily business wouldn't get off to the best start.

Next, she would unlatch the front door noisily. Not finding the milk packets usually delivered at the doorstep, she'd call the store again and order milk in her loudest voice. I'd burrow into my pillow, trying to drown the sounds out. I recall my annoyance with a twinge of guilt.

Now there is silence, the air sterile. I gulp, my sobs rising from a deep place. This is what the beginning of a life without Amma feels like. Standing in her kitchen, I stare around me. Every pot and pan has an Amma story etched on it. These are her dishes, the stainless steel bowls in which she served cardamom-flavoured payasam every festival day, the copper-bottomed pot which doled out several servings of rasam, the *davara* (a small steel bowl) in which she cooled milk for Appa. Her hands wrapped around these glasses and mugs, scrubbed the skillet on which she made hundreds of crisp, golden dosas for Sunday breakfasts. Her DNA is still here. The thought sends a chill through me.

It strikes me that the pots and pans in the kitchen look as orphaned as we do. Wiping my eyes, I set about the task of making coffee. I can't find the sugar bowl; I don't know where she stored the coffee powder.

Triggers abound. The house is full of her; she is everywhere.

All this time, I've avoided going into my parents' bedroom. It would feel akin to stepping on an emotional landmine. But I can't dodge it any more. If I don't cross over that barrier, how am I going to persuade Appa?

I take baby steps into the room, a toddler on wobbly legs. I sit on her bed. I curl up, fetus-like, and sob into Amma's pillow that still smells of her hair oil and the ointment she used on her sore neck. Right across from me on the dresser, her cosmetics: turmeric cream, talcum powder, hair oil, her bangles and packets of maroon-coloured bindis. Her bed was always much too crowded, the narrow space beside her stack of pillows stuffed with her pain ointment, her inhaler, scarves and a stack of Tamil magazines.

I spy her grey diary and flip it open to a random page. It is filled with her slanted writing: grocery lists, lists of clothes sent for ironing, medicines to order, phone numbers, payments made and due. On a fresh page is a chart my brother-in-law devised to record her fluid intake when she was diagnosed with jaundice. I see that Amma has been meticulous in updating the information.

Her well-worn slippers with their familiar indentations sit

obediently beside the bed. It's all too much. How ironic that these everyday objects have assumed sentimental status overnight, mementoes of an individual, irreplaceable in value.

There's her closet, with all her saris. How will I exorcise the demons that lurk in there? I'm afraid to open it and be assaulted by her smells.

My sister-in-law finds me and attempts to comfort me. She tells me my mother is in a better place. Her intentions are noble, but it feels like a mocking lie. I don't know if Amma is in a better place. Amma's 'better place' was always where her family was.

I look around me, try to find Amma in the things she used. Each item is now an obstacle on the life journey we have to go on, without her.

Is it even possible to contemplate a time when I will breathe normally? Will there be a day in the distant future when I think of Amma and feel a sense of peace that she's been delivered from her suffering?

For now, I miss her with everything in me. And I miss her even more every time I look at Appa.

11

$\mathcal{G}$IRISH AND RUKI ARE EXPECTED TO ARRIVE IN CHENNAI the following day. Girish's business trip to Chennai had already been planned and his tickets booked well in advance of Amma's passing.

Days, nights, dates are all a blur. My mind is muddied, swirling, awash in grief. So, when Girish calls, all I'm expecting is a long-distance hug and I love you. I'm totally unprepared for what he tells me. A snowstorm has delayed their British Airways flight. My husband and daughter are stuck at Manchester airport and are clueless at this time about their ETA in Chennai.

I listen to my husband rant about the 'clots' a.k.a. customer service personnel at Heathrow. How they parrot well-rehearsed apologies unmindful of passenger inconvenience, blah, blah, blah. He goes on and on, a long diatribe about serpentine queues, lack of hot water in the hotel bathroom, lost bags, the chaotic hotel lobby and enraged passengers, blah, blah, blah.

Nothing sticks in my brain. It's a heavy sponge, overloaded with emotion, unable to absorb any more. So I do to him what I've often accused him of doing to me – listen uninterestedly.

After a complex process of re-routing and flying across several time zones, Girish and Ruki arrive in Chennai, four days later. I meet them at the airport. The first order of business is driving to the store to buy underwear, since their bags are stuck somewhere in Dubai.

At home, Ruki takes her first hot shower in four days. When she steps out of the bathroom, her skin actually looks a couple of shades lighter.

The population explosion at my parents' is enough to make China look good. Girish and I decide to spend the night at the company guesthouse.

12

*I*T IS STRANGE, THIS FEELING. WITH AMMA GONE, I FEEL LIKE I don't have a home any more. This has always been home, but now I feel homeless. The one home that's always remained a constant in my life has changed forever. It comes to me, the realization that it isn't the house, but the mother who makes it one.

Ruki's friend's mother calls to offer condolences. She asks me over. I politely decline. She badgers, insists I'll feel better if I get out of the house. I want to push her away, scream: *Nothing will make me feel better.* But I swallow the fury rising in my chest and say, yes I'll go, knowing I won't.

When I set the phone down, Girish asks about visiting our ex-neighbours in the condo where we lived. They called, offered condolences, invited us over, he says.

'I don't want to go,' I protest.

'Why? They're just being kind.'

'I just don't want to go.'

'It's just a visit. It'll help take your mind off this … We don't have to stay long. Just half an hour or so …' he negotiates.

'You go. I'm not going anywhere,' I hold firm.

'But why?'

'I just don't *want* to go anywhere. I want to stay right here.'

My husband shakes his head and makes a face, the one that says I don't know why you have to be so stubborn about something as simple as a neighbourly visit.

What he doesn't know, what I don't know how to explain, is that I don't want to take my mind off this sadness, this misery that's eating me up. It's the only way I know how to stay close to

Amma. Leaving Amma's home is simply not an option. I need to stay close to Appa, Maya and Mahesh, the people I share this pain with. Weird though it sounds, pain is the anesthetic I need to stay numb right now.

The only people I will even consider visiting is Amma's family because I know Amma is there in some intangible, ephemeral way.

—<·><><·>—

On the home front, things slide downhill. A much-needed discussion about Amma's finances ends up as a mud-slinging session. We're back to our familiar formations: my brother ranged against the rest of us. All the debris that lies just below the surface spews out. He hurls heated words. *You abandoned Appa and Amma by moving to America. You've always been concerned only about your life. You took decisions about Appa's health that I knew nothing about and never agreed to.*

He storms out of the room. His words stay longer and cut to the core. It's like an auto rewind-and-play button in my head. *You abandoned … You left … You decided …*

The following days are fraught with tension. Petty matters like missing keys and Appa's medicine doses become artillery for rapid-fire exchanges. Accusations and finger-pointing ensue. The air is charged.

I'm shocked at how quickly it has all unravelled. I thought my equation with my brother was finally back on track. It took eight months of careful stitching us all back together, but days after Amma's passing, the relationships are ragged.

It is another layer of sadness, like losing him all over again. I keep communication to a bare minimum – my grief is too raw. Exposing myself to any other kind of attack intensifies my fear of being alone. I'm despondent that this time of mourning, of coming together has split us apart in the most frightening and despicable way. What would Amma say? She died, comforted in knowing that her warring children had finally declared a truce. And now, just days later, everything is in tatters.

To make matters and my mood worse, I'm expecting my period. In some parts of India, a menstruating woman is still considered 'impure' and must stay away from significant functions like weddings, religious rites and temple visits during those days. The rituals surrounding death are considered especially sacred. That means if I start my period I cannot visit the temple where the first series of rites will be performed every morning for the next five days.

My aunt optimistically starts me on a pill, an attempt to delay my period. All I need is a week's reprieve to sneak past the rituals. I swallow the pill with half a glass of water and a gallon of trepidation. This has never worked in the past: Not at my uncle's wedding, festival days, and other religious occasions. My period has a mind of its own; it has always showed up on schedule.

This time is no different. End result: I miss all the rituals. Isolation, all over again. My heart aches. *May be Amma didn't want me there or she would've fixed this.* I feel excluded, an outcast. My mind tricks me into believing Amma could have influenced this and created a positive outcome. She knows how many family functions I've had to sit out.

That said, a part of me breathes easy. On some level, I'm relieved to be spared the responsibility of participating in a series of rituals I barely understand. I'm more comfortable grieving in a manner that feels right to me.

When you have your period, the kitchen and altar are off-limits. You're not allowed physical contact with others, either. Someone will have to serve me meals and wash my dishes. It's the adult version of being sent to Coventry.

I decide to make life easy for all by moving into my cousin, Ginny's, home for a couple of days. The atmosphere in her home is the closest to normal living that I've had in the past ten days. Her boisterous, fun-loving daughters aged nine and six are just the company I need. Hanging out with them and laughing about silly stuff is therapeutic. Ginny is a whiz in the kitchen and loves dishing up mouth-watering meals. For the first time in two weeks, I taste a meal and sleep a full eight hours at night.

The first series of rites are done; the more elaborate ceremonies are due to begin two days from now. The first ceremony is performed on the tenth day after a person's passing. The thirteenth day marks the finale. An elaborate feast follows the rituals in which close friends and family participate.

When I return home from Ginny's, Maya and I start making lists: invitees, groceries, items for the rituals and caterer. We update the phone book, invite friends and relatives, and contact the two priests who will perform the rites. We buy new clothes for us all; tradition dictates that we must visit the temple, attired in new clothes on the day of the final ceremonies.

The upshot of this is that I feel completely unsettled. I'm unfamiliar with the religious aspects of death and dying and am having trouble negotiating that territory. When it came to all things religious, Amma was usually the one in charge. With her gone, we're rudderless, wandering around, clumsily bumping into one another.

Animosity in the air is an energy drain. Mahesh and his wife continue to keep to themselves. Conversations are clipped, and happen only when absolutely necessary. Sullen silences, terse responses and lack of eye contact are challenging at a time when we should bond and honour Amma's spirit.

Their toddler is the only tension-reliever. When he tears around the living room wiggling his diapered bottom, yogurt-rice smeared all over his face, we have to drop our stupid defences and laugh.

I've been assigned the task of composing Amma's obituary. The obituary is for a national newspaper, a public announcement of Amma's passing.

I'm honoured and frightened all at once. Pen in hand, I stare at an empty sheet of paper, blank. My head feels hollowed out, the words have disappeared. And I'm supposed to be the one that can craft and create word-magic, even if someone shook me awake at midnight and handed me a pen.

How do I condense forty-four years of what Amma meant to me in a 6x12cm obituary? Over the next hour, I write and overwrite, write and tear, write and scratch some more. No words are adequate to contain her beautiful, gentle spirit. But like all writing assignments, the deadline looms ahead so I must come up with something that sounds reasonably sane.

When I eventually do, it has the feel of a poem. I read it aloud to my siblings who play editors, and we come up with a finished piece which leaves a lot unsaid.

The sole comfort in the exercise is this: I pay a final tribute to my mother through words, a wordsmith she birthed and nurtured.

13

$\mathcal{I}$T IS 7 FEBRUARY, ELEVEN DAYS AFTER AMMA's passing. THE most significant death ceremonies begin tomorrow. However, the priests arrive to do some of the prep work today.

Vijaya Mami cooks a special meal, and close family partakes in the feast.

On the following day, about fifty people arrive early in the day to participate in the ceremonies and stay for lunch. The two priests chant for hours, wave smoking incense sticks around, and feed the sacred fire with copious amounts of ghee. Amma smiles from inside a garlanded photo frame, a genial smile frozen forever.

The air is thick with smoke; heady scents of camphor, burning ghee and jasmine permeate the room. Every time I look at Amma's garlanded photo, a shiver goes through me; trapped behind a photo frame, she is reduced to a memory.

The head priest expounds on the meaning of the mystical chants. Amma died at quarter to ten on a Tuesday night when all the stars were aligned right, he explains to the congregation. Her soul will ascend to the heavens, he confirms, in the manner of an experienced tour guide who's played escort to the departed.

All those who love Amma – cousins, cousins-in-law, nephews, friends, sisters-in-law and neighbours – are here wearing their best silks and somber expressions. The only one missing is Appa.

Complaining of a pain in his right hip, Appa has not even showered today. In fact, he is still in bed. I've coaxed and cajoled since morning, tried to get him up, showered and dressed. As the ceremonies progress, I pop into his room to check on him periodically.

'Appa, it's not too late. Go take a quick bath and come sit with us,' I say.

He says nothing, just stubbornly shakes his head.

'Please, Appa. We're all here. Everyone is asking about you.'

He shuts his eyes tight, to say *leave me alone*.

It's the ultimate irony of tradition, I think. The man Amma was married to for forty-seven years, the man who was her soulmate, has no part to play in the rituals surrounding her death. If he were required to perform some of the rites, I know Appa would be up, clad in a crisp white gold-bordered dhoti, holy ash generously smeared across his forehead.

I need to be out there, welcoming guests and attending to the priests' requests for white rice, more ghee, lotus petals, and turmeric sticks. But I feel torn. I want to sit beside Appa, hold his hand, stroke his back, help ease whatever he's struggling with. When I gently prod, he remains mute. It is only when his sister – almost two decades older than him – arrives, that his anguish cracks wide open and the floodwaters gush out. He breaks down and sobs like a child in her arms.

In the evening, we dress up in our new clothes, visit Marundeeswarar Temple and hand over containers of leftover food from the morning's feast to a local charity.

That night, Girish plays the diplomat and initiates peace talks amongst us siblings. Both he and I are tense that Maya may erupt. She is only a year younger than Mahesh; they had always been close. His fresh betrayal has cut really deep, and she is easily provoked to bitter recriminations. She's also the most fragile, having been up close to the trauma, starting with Amma's diagnosis eight months ago.

Fortunately, things go smoothly. Maya keeps her anger in check. We promise to make a concerted effort to focus on the big picture and Appa, even if we don't see eye to eye.

My husband strikes a chord with his final words: 'Let's take away the most important virtue of Amma's life – she would've tried peace for all under any circumstances.'

14

$\mathcal{O}$VER THE NEXT COUPLE OF DAYS, WE CALL IN-HOME NURSING care centres to locate a nurse for Appa's full-time care. Luckily, a nurse is available.

Maya receives her at the train station and brings her home. One look at this unsmiling stranger and my heart sinks. My hunch is borne out in a matter of hours. Appa minces no words in expressing his strong dislike towards her, swats her away like a pesky fly, and orders her out of sight.

Last evening, waiting in a doctor's office, Appa told me that Mahesh had had a chat with him. Mahesh plans to quit his job in Chicago and move his family back to India so Appa can move in with them. Both Maya and Guru have full-time jobs, and Maya travels on the job. Hiring a full-time nurse for Appa's care is an unacceptable option to Mahesh, as he told Appa.

Tradition dictates that aged parents are a son's responsibility. I feel grateful that my brother is being a man, shouldering the duty of caring for a bereaved parent, even if it means he has to move continents. It is a cherished Indian custom, one that many sons honour. However, with modern globalization and the break-up of the joint family system, most have not always been able to deliver. Caught between a doddering parent and the dollar sign, they have begun to struggle to make a choice.

So, when Appa makes his scary eyes and yells at the nurse to get out of the room, I try to calm him down. I remind him that this is only a stopgap arrangement until Mahesh moves back.

'I don't want her here. Tell her to go. I can take care of myself,' Appa purses his lips, a petulant toddler.

'You can't, Appa. She's here only to help you. Serve you meals and make sure you take your medicines,' I try.

'I can go into the kitchen and cook my own meals. I don't need any one to serve me.'

I give up this futile line of reasoning. The poor man is incapable of logic, thanks to a damaged prefrontal cortex. Unlike toddlers who orbit their mothers and stay a safe distance from strangers, Appa's modus operandi is to scare them away with bad behaviour. Appa has always had a part-time nurse. He has the honour of getting three nurses to quit, so the behaviour is self-rewarding, one he has no qualms about using when a threat looms on his horizon. One time, he waved a broom at a nurse to indicate that he'd whack her if she didn't leave him alone. All those times, Amma was around to step in and make peace. Of course, Appa used this to his advantage by demanding that she cater to his every need, nurse or no nurse.

⋘◦◦◦⋙

It is two weeks since Amma died. I still blanch when referring to her in the past tense.

Explosive tempers have been wreaking havoc at home, but one afternoon I walk in on a strange incident.

It appears the pressure-cooker wanted a piece of the action too. Fragrant pilaf is splattered across the floor, the ceiling and kitchen counters. Mixed in with the rice are shards of glass from the light bulb it crashed into.

Vijaya Mami is standing in the corner, trembling like an earthquake survivor. Maya and I take the lead in cleaning up the mess. Once Mami's nerves calm down, she pitches in and then cooks lunch from scratch.

At this point, after-life communication is a subject I know nothing of. It is much later that I encounter literature on the world of mediums.

But Sheri, my writer-friend back in Chicago, often talked of the events in the days and weeks following her dad's passing. She believes that spirits who have crossed over will do anything to get the attention of loved ones left behind; they turn on televisions and light bulbs to show us they're still involved in our lives.

It makes me stop and wonder. Was that Amma in an exploding pressure cooker? I could never combine Amma and explosion in the same sentence; she is the gentlest soul I know. May be she had to resort to desperate measures to make us notice. I'll never know. At least, not until I get to wherever she is.

⋖⋗

Maya and I begin the unsavoury task of ferreting in Amma's many handbags and excavating her investment documents. Amma wasn't a believer in files, which makes our job as chancy as an Easter egg hunt. We file everything we find and head off to my uncle's house to hand them over. Appa had played the role of financial adviser most of their married life. Ever since his accident, Amma had leaned on her brother to funnel the money into reliable investments that promise good returns and handle all the paperwork.

Amma came into a small fortune about three years ago, when Grandpa passed away. Little did she or any of us know how timely that inheritance was. A big chunk of it paid for her cancer treatment.

As we're preparing to leave, Mahesh informs me that he's flying back to Chicago later in the evening. It's eleven in the morning, and I'm somewhat thrown by this abrupt announcement, but I'm learning to take his behavioural quirks in stride. My sister-in-law and nephew will stay on in Chennai a couple of days, then fly to her parents' home in another town.

The battle lines between him and Maya are now well-defined, so I promise Mahesh I'll escort his wife and child to the airport to see them off.

I'm overcome by emotion when Mahesh takes leave, and this

surprises me. He looks at my teary eyed, holds me for what feels like too short a time. No matter what, we've all been living under the same roof, sharing in this awful time, forging some kind of a tenuous bond, a new normal. Amma's passing – no matter our differences – is a connecting thread in our lives. In Mahesh's leaving for Chicago, the adage – life must go on – becomes reality. Our fragile family is splitting up again. Somehow, it feels like another loss.

Two days later, my sister-in-law and nephew leave. When I return from the airport, the silence in the house is deafening. Without my little nephew's lively chatter, this has become a void, a stark reminder of a family in mourning.

We're not just mourning Amma; we're mourning the passing of a way of life as we knew it.

15

$\mathcal{I}$T IS 14 FEBRUARY, VALENTINE'S DAY. RUKI AND I ARE scheduled to fly back to Chicago tonight. Girish has two more weeks of business in India.

Around eleven in the morning we visit Paati's house to take leave of the family. Sadness wells up in me when I hear Paati's frail voice whisper 'Bon Voyage'. Everything feels impermanent and shaky. I can't help wondering if I'll see her again.

Our next stop is the company guest house where Girish, Ruki and I have been staying nights so the pressure on space is relieved to some extent at my parents' home. We eat a late lunch, pack our bags, and take a short nap.

Late afternoon, we load our luggage into the taxi and drive to my parents' home. The plan is to leave for the airport from there.

Outside the taxi window, life goes on. It's a hot, muggy day. Sitting in the air-conditioned confines of the taxi, I watch labourers hauling bricks and water at construction sites, their black bodies glistening with sweat, vendors shouting at the tops of their voices, hawking their wares. Everyone doing what they have to do with what they have.

I step out of the taxi and walk inside Seashore Apartments. Appa is sitting in the living room, reading a newspaper. The nurse is sprawled on a mat on the floor, fast asleep. This is what the future looks like – him and the nurse – I think to myself. Everything in me wants to stay back in Chennai, keep him safe.

'Hi, Appa,' I say.

He smiles at me, turns to the sports page.

A little later, I watch him struggle with the buttons on the TV remote. Amma was his TV fixer-repairer, always just a holler away.

Much more accessible than the technician who needed several reminder calls a day before he finally showed up just when they'd settle down for an afternoon nap.

Amma figured out the trick of getting the TV to cooperate through a process of trial and error. Most times just pushing a random bunch of buttons or jiggling a couple of wires restored the connection like magic. One time, I remember seeing her whack the remote control against the palm of her hand rather violently. When I expressed my concern at her maltreatment of sensitive electronic devices, she cheerfully reassured me that it had never failed to work. Sure enough, seconds later, the TV screen blinked to life, and Appa was one happy camper.

I mimic the process now, feeling like a complete idiot. Nothing happens. I send up a silent prayer to Amma. *Help me get this thing to work.* Clearly, she hears me and re-jigs the malfunctioning wires from wherever she is. Satisfied, Appa leans back and gives himself over to the world of tennis.

Hours before I leave, I sit in front of Amma's closet and stare at her gorgeous collection of saris and jewellery. This was Amma's one weakness. She had a special fondness for Bengal cotton saris, pearls and colourful precious stones. I open one jewellery box after another, sift through ear-studs and bead necklaces that graced her at weddings, festive occasions and family get-togethers.

Thinking back to July last year, a moment presents itself. It was the evening before my departure to Chicago. She placed a handful of ear-studs in my palm saying, 'Here, take these. I don't think I'll be using them any more.' Did she have a premonition, one she didn't share with any one?

Amma's zest for life is her most precious legacy, a gift I will always cherish. It never ceased to amaze me how, on the morning of her chemo, she'd sit on her bed and carefully sort through her jewellery. Delicately, she'd slide out a necklace to match her sari and head scarf. Looking good was important even on days when she didn't feel good.

Maya comes into the room. 'Take whatever you like,' she says. 'Remember how much she loved this purple sari?' I say. 'She kept looking for a matching necklace, and was so happy when she found one. She actually called to tell me.'

Maya sighs. We look at each other, hold hands.

I tell Maya I'd like to take Amma's glasses, two saris, a faded nightgown she often wore, and one of her scarves. It tears me up to think this is all I have of her now.

A voice says: *You have much more than that.*

I ignore the voice; I don't believe it.

Soon, we set the table for dinner. I pick at my food, a million things crowding my head, anxiety and worry clouding everything.

Before saying goodbye, I touch my forehead to Appa's feet to take his blessing. Maya, Guru, Girish, Ruki and I get inside the car. Appa stands in the doorway, a frail figure held up by a cane, hand raised in a feeble wave. The nurse is standing right behind him.

I think back to earlier that evening and the reverence with which he lit two joss sticks and placed them in the altar right in front of Amma's photo frame. Then he draped a string of jasmine around her photo, flowers he'd carefully chosen from the flower-seller who came to the door every evening.

It overwhelms me, the feeling that I'm abandoning Appa. It makes me want to run into his arms and hold him tight, promise that I'll keep him safe. But I have to go. Suddenly, I'm reminded that this is how Amma wanted it. This is why she guarded the truth of her terminal illness, so we could move to America and begin our new life.

At the airport, Girish holds me tight. I cling to him, daunted by the fear of two weeks in Chicago without him by my side. Cupping my face in his hands, my husband whispers, 'I'll be with you very soon. Hang in there.'

My lips tremble. These days, I get teary at the smallest act of kindness, the tiniest gesture of tenderness. Next, I hug Maya really hard, wishing I didn't have to go.

'Take care of yourself,' I say. 'Remember, I'm just a phone call away.'

She turns away from me, tears spilling down her cheeks.

Why is everything so different? Why? Why?

My little sister is donning the mantle of parental responsibility all over again, a task we've shared for a decade.

———<∙∙∙∙>———

Half an hour later, Ruki and I are checked in, another long journey starting from Chennai, through Mumbai and culminating in Chicago.

When we disembark at Mumbai airport, it's around half-past eight at night. The airport is in the throes of renovation. Long lines snake towards a makeshift security counter. The passengers, a lost, bewildered lot, are being herded to their appropriate counters by a posse of uniformed officials.

My feet are killing me, my head hurts, and my eyes are raw from days and nights of crying.

After checking our bags in, we have to endure a three-hour wait before takeoff. I'm so exhausted I slump into a bright orange plastic chair. Ruki is wide awake, and hunkers down with a voluminous book. I feel bad to leave her to her own devices, but I have nothing to offer by way of conversation.

I'm brimful of emotion, heavy, saturated. Nothing matters any more. I don't know what I'm doing in Mumbai airport in the middle of the night, lights blazing around me. All I wanted was to stay in Chennai, and fester in the cocoon of sorrow. In some irrational way, leaving India feels like snipping the umbilical cord; every fibre of my being resists it. I'm not ready to let Amma go. I'm not ready to leave India. And yet, go I must, insists the realist inside my head: Because Ruki cannot miss more than ten days of school; because I have to be the responsible parent; because Girish is still in India; because Amma is gone, and is never coming back; because life must go on; and on and on, my mind spews out a string of becauses.

The rest of the journey is a numbed blur: tasteless meals, threatening tears, and terrible, bottomless grief.

Ruki is very quiet. I guess my overt display of emotion in the past two weeks has thrown her. She's never seen me like this before. One doesn't always know what's going on inside my daughter's head or heart – unless she chooses to share it. In this respect, she's just like her dad; his DNA is deeply embedded in her – she's calm, contained and controlled.

I often think of her as a wise soul who has come into this world with astute affirmations like *this too shall pass, live and let live,* and *don't sweat the small stuff* coded into her genes. As a toddler, she would go into a store, gaze wistfully at a doll, and mouth the words: *This doll is beautiful, but I know I can't have it because it's too expensive.* As a teenager, her stock response to her parents' suggestion to buy a new pair of shoes is *why do I need another pair?* Most times, I believe she'd do a great job of parenting me. This is one of those moments. I'm so grateful she's with me, and gracious enough to offer me the gift of her undemanding presence.

Twenty-some hours later, we finally touch down at O'Hare. It is seven in the evening. After immigration formalities, we haul our bags off the baggage carousel, flag a cab and head home.

The bleak winter landscape, snowdrifts piled on the side of the road, and frigid February cold underscore my dreary mood.

Moments after we get home, the doorbell rings. It's my friend Rajini's husband, with a loaf of bread and a half gallon of milk. It strikes me then that my refrigerator is empty and the first task ahead of me is grocery shopping. The very thought is pressure, like a Sumo wrestler squatting on my chest. Such is the debilitating nature of grief, as I will come to realize in the weeks and months to follow. I thank my friend's husband – who meets my befuddled expression, not knowing what to say – and shut the door.

I plod into the kitchen. Staring into an empty refrigerator is enough to make me feel utterly alone. I ache for the familiarity of India. Someone would call the store for groceries to be home-delivered. Or a maid would go shop for me. Or one among my million relatives would send food home. Here, I have to do this all alone.

Girish, my rock, who's held me through some of the most difficult times in my life, is a continent away. I feel such an intense need for him, for Amma. It's a gnawing ache that starts in the pit of my belly and consumes me.

I do the only thing I can: I drag the covers over my head and pray for sleep to come find me.

16

SLIDING INTO A DEEP SLEEP, I STEAL MOMENTS OF PEACE. But somewhere in the murky light of night, fitful dreams sneak in: Amma is writhing in pain, she's screaming, she's being wheeled away on a gurney, I am screaming. Finally , the nightmares release me from their clutch. A delicious inertia claims me in the pre-dawn hours. When I eventually awaken, grief rushes at me: fresh, raw and real. I shut my eyes tight, lose Amma all over again.

It's Sunday morning. I wander around the apartment, an untethered balloon, directionless, lost and floating. I didn't know a two-bedroom apartment with two people in it could feel so desolate. Our apartment is well-heated, but I'm shivering uncontrollably.

The phone is silent. I haven't made any friends here, mostly acquaintances. But then, we've only been in Chicago nine months, and I've spent two of those in India. Not a lot of time to cultivate a social circuit, plus I wasn't really very sociable, with my life turned upside down. No one really knows me. No one knew my mother. It is a painfully lonely place to be in.

I gravitate to my laptop and open my e-mail. It is the quickest connection to Chennai, the only place I really want to be.

A snowstorm of condolence messages drifts into my inbox.

An aunt writes: '… losing a loved mother makes us feel orphaned, as if we are cast out alone in the world …'

'I'm sure words are pretty meaningless under the circumstances, but I do hope you find the strength and acceptance to cope …' from an editor friend.

'What a sad time for you, especially being so far away from

her ... I'm sorry that you cannot come back as a tutor this semester ...' writes my ESL supervisor.

'Perhaps God was kind enough not to let her suffer too long ...' a well-loved teacher writes.

A friend, my pregnancy buddy (she and I had our babies a few weeks apart) writes, '... I went through the same experience in 2001 with my Ma. I am almost crying now, feeling your grief and recounting mine ... now I can see Ma's smiling picture every morning and think fondly of the angel I had (and still have) in my life ... it will be the same with you ...'

But the next two e-mails punch me with the power of profound loss.

A friend from Madison writes, '... I can only imagine that it must hurt like hell, particularly since you are not only far, far away, you are also in a place lacking in the comfort of friends and family, others that you know and are familiar with ... time marches on, inexorable and unyielding, proving we are ourselves just ephemeral, proving that we should not take ourselves nor our beliefs too seriously, instead focusing on our lives now ... I have no idea if you can drive up here, but if you care to, you are always welcome. You know the place, the house, the room. Come here for laughter, arguments, music, food, wine and some reading ...'

A grade school friend writes, 'I remember your mother as being strikingly beautiful, direct and very simple. She exuded genuine warmth and was quick to laugh ... when I met her after your father's accident, she was strong and optimistic ... if there is one legacy that she left you, it is the attitude of practical determination and hope in the face of adversity ... when we mourn the dead we actually mourn the living. We mainly grieve for our own selves, our loss of identity. After all, they were the most powerful influence in defining the kind of people we are for the rest of our lives. We suddenly feel incomplete ... Here is a line that stays with me from ninth grade when I first read it, and helps me cope with death: "To live in the hearts and deeds of those left behind is not to die" – Harold Robbins, *A Stone for Danny Fisher.*'

I drop my head into my hands and cry. Here are the people who knew how Amma looked, smelt and smiled. Here I am, in a country where she has zero context, where she is anonymous.

——< †⊙† †⊙† >——

Late morning, Ruki and I drive to Dominick's. We usually shop at Meijer, but if I have to pay a few extra dollars to shop and drive less than a mile on treacherous snowy roads, I'll do it. I walk into Dominick's thinking, *I just lost my mother. What do I need apples for?*

A well-dressed lady is standing at the fruit bin. She picks up an apple, inspects it, tosses it back on the pile, then picks another. She repeats the process with clementines and pears. I watch her from a safe distance, hypnotized, utterly impressed by her efficiency. Then I take my place in front of the bin and stare at the fruit. They all look the same. Colours and shapes and textures blend and blur. I pick an apple. It feels heavy in my palm. I smell it. Nothing. I turn it around, then watch it sit in the middle of my palm before I chuck it back on the pile. I don't know what to do; I don't know how to do this. The simple act of buying fruit which once took me all of three minutes has become a chore of Sisyphean proportions.

Ruki comes to my rescue. She says nothing, simply slides out the grocery list through my limp fingers and starts to crisscross the aisle in determined strides, grabbing bread and cereal, detergent and low-fat yogurt. I push the cart, follow her around. That I know how to do.

On the drive home, the air is thick with silence. I'm the conversationalist in the family. When I stop talking, our apartment turns into a tomb. I'm usually chatty with Ruki, teasing, sharing stories in the safe, intimate way you can only with your daughter. Now, I sense that Ruki is at odds. She doesn't quite know how to bridge the gap, or what might be appropriate conversation, given my mental state. I, on the other hand, have no energy and nothing to say.

When we get home, I open the door of the freezer. Girish has stocked it with boxes and boxes of store-bought vegetarian meals. I've always cooked meals from scratch; I'm not used to eating pre-cooked food out of a box. But this one time I'm truly grateful for the indulgence. I peel the foil off a couple of boxes, stick them in the microwave. Ruki has to eat, even if I left my appetite back in India.

17

*M*ONDAY MORNING, RUKI WAKES UP TO HER ALARM CLOCK, gets dressed and trudges out the door at the ungodly hour of quarter-past six, her backpack weighing her down. I imagine she is relieved to leave the grave atmosphere of home and travel to her fun world of giggly, chattering teenagers where her most traumatic moment could be being penalized for a forgotten ID badge. It's a world she can slide into with a known ease, and pretend all is right with her universe – at least for a few hours. No such luxuries are available to me.

After seeing Ruki off, a furious game of ping-pong plays out inside my head: *I don't want to go to work. I have to go to work. Do I really want to go into a building full of sickly old folks? How can I go to work feeling like this? I can't hide forever. I just got this job and I've been gone for two weeks already.*

The mental back-and-forth is enough to exhaust me. I slump into the living room armchair, defeated even before I've begun.

I have no idea what moved me from that enervating place to dressed-in-black-pants-and-blue-polo uniform and behind the wheel of my Corolla, but I find myself there. It's a little unsettling that I have no memory of taking a shower (or not), eating breakfast (or not), locking the front door (or not). Thank God I've come to before I turned on the ignition.

The leather of the steering wheel is cold under my fingers. I close my eyes, drag a breath in and try to do a mental MapQuest. Slowly, I take my foot off the brake pedal and watch the car move forward.

I've been driving less than four months, and this is my first

Chicago winter. Every time I'm behind the wheel, my stomach muscles twist. The Chennai memory of arguing with arrogant auto-rickshaw drivers for a reduced fare makes me nostalgic today.

Girish is so far away. I stare at the endless landscape of grey, the colours sucked out of everything, and feel fresh terror. Tears pool in my eyes. *This is so unfair. Life is so unfair.*

I think back to nine months ago when our family picture was intact. That picture lies in shards today, and I can do nothing to put the pieces back together. I feel like someone should've told me this was coming. Why didn't I see this coming? But what would I have done if someone had come up and said to me, 'You need to prepare yourself for the worst.' Most likely, chewed a piece of their head off, or cut them out of my life for being a prophet of doom.

Focus, focus.

I force myself to pay attention to the lights and traffic. The last thing I need is a fender-bender. I wouldn't even know what to do, whom to call. Rajini is the closest I have to a friend. Rajini, who's a whole decade younger, inhabits the world of swing sets, play dates and Barbie doll birthday cakes, an alternate universe as far as I'm concerned.

I feel like I don't have a single friend here.

Outside the car window, tree after tree stands naked, forlorn, shorn of its colourful drapery. The loneliness is like a fist that squeezes tight around my heart. I drive slowly, deliberately, convinced that I've forgotten my way to The Palms, the senior living community where I have a part-time job. I'd been working just three weeks when I left for India, but that seems like a lifetime ago.

I drive past dirty mounds of snow piled along the sidewalks, ease into the lot and park. I clutch the steering wheel, unwilling to let go. I don't want to step inside that building and face all those looks and words of sympathy.

When the cold starts to creep into my bones, I climb out of the car, huddle into my red jacket and plod towards the entrance, trying to hold my fragile self together. Not too many people know me yet.

—⟨ ❀ ❀ ⟩—

Every Monday morning is the Connect 101 presentation, an hour-long PowerPoint on a topical subject. The spectrum ranges from 'Christmas Traditions' and 'Mardi Gras' to the 'World's Best Travel Destinations' and 'Better Brain Health'. The presentation is held in a large, well-lit room with chandeliers glittering overhead.

Lori, my supervisor, is the presenter. Nervousness aflutter in my belly, I walk into the lecture room, and straight into Lori's open arms. She holds me tight. When we pull apart she looks me in the eye and asks, 'How're you doing?'

I look away, feeling the pressure in the back of my throat. Then I shrug, non-committal, unable to speak.

'I'm so sorry,' she says, as I fix my gaze on the patterns of the bright red carpet at my feet.

Usually, about twenty to thirty residents hobble in with their walkers or roll in their wheelchairs, a precious few unaided, before settling in to listen and watch.

The residents are shuffling in. The ones that know me come up and give me a hug. News has spread. 'So sorry,' they mumble. Others cluster around them and ask, 'What happened?'

'She lost her mom,' some say softly, for they are not words one shouts. But the loud 'Whaat?' from the hearing-impaired prompt them to turn up the volume on my mother's death. '*Who* died?' others are still trying to hear. And decorum be damned when the know-alls now shout, 'Her mother died.' 'Oh,' say those who hear this time. Some are still trying to piece it together from their neighbours. I stand on the sidelines and watch the story of Amma's death become an improv show.

I feel their pity pouring all over me. I don't want their pity. I want Amma.

Soon, Lori is all business and hands me a sheaf of forms. I need to update the forms with resident information so we can use it as a reference for the 'Residents Photo Directory' we're compiling tomorrow. She has to repeat the instructions three times to me before it sinks in.

I stand in the middle of the room, the forms limp in my hand, the seniors in the middle of their walker wars – *I got here first, move yours over to that side, I have no room* – everything fading, blurring, then coming into sharp focus. It's like my mind's zoom feature is going crazy. What am I doing here? Who are all these people?

My *mother* just died.

Four life-changing words, the only words that are relevant above the din in the room. Any way you arrange them, the effect is the same: heartbreak.

Thankfully, in a while, the lights dim, the whispers in the room hush and the big screen comes to life. I sink into a chair, grateful for the reprieve. Five minutes later, the Chicagoland manager, Wendy, taps me on the shoulder and whispers, 'Dave wants to see you.'

I tiptoe to the back of the room where Dave Walsh, the community's executive director, gathers me in a hug. 'I'm so sorry for your loss,' he whispers, and it takes every ounce of willpower to hold my tears back. There are some occasions in life when you're thankful for the low visibility in a dimly-lit room.

When the presentation is over, I record the seniors' personal information on the forms and hand the forms over to Lori. I'm not sure what to do next. Our programme is just about taking shape in the community, and we don't have a well-choreographed work routine. The computers for the seventh-floor lab haven't arrived yet. Wendy, Lori and I traipse back to the lone computer in the game room, our temporary headquarters.

A short young man of average build strolls in. Wendy smiles, and exchanges pleasantries before turning to us. 'Meet Andy,' she says. 'He's joining our team as a computer lab assistant.'

Andy has friendly brown eyes and a gentle manner. We shake hands and I welcome him into the fold. Wendy suggests to Andy that he shadow me for a few days: watch me working with the seniors and get familiar with the Connect 101 website. We set up a time to work together the following day.

———

That evening I'm sitting in the living room, my thoughts far away, when Ruki comes to me.

'Ma,' she starts, tentative. 'I really don't like leaving you alone at home. I can drop out of the play. I mean … it's not like I'm in it or anything. I'm just the Stud Ass., Ms Smith will find someone else.'

Even with all that's going on, I can't help but smile at *Stud Ass*, the Fremd theatre crowd's lingo for student assistant.

'Absolutely not. No way,' I protest. 'This is your big dream, Ruk. I can't let you do that.'

'But I won't get home till six or even seven most evenings. And it'll be, like, even later as we get closer to tech week.'

'Yeah, but Dad will be back in Chicago by then.'

'What happens when he has to travel again?' she cocks her head to a side.

She's been giving this some thought.

'Ruki, I love how concerned you are about me, but you don't have to do this. I can—'

'—Mama, you're going to be all by yourself from the time you get back from work until I get home. I don't know. I just feel …' She shrugs, uncomfortable about articulating her fear at what might befall her mother, if left unwatched.

She has a point. I usually get home between half-past twelve and one in the afternoon. I'll have to rattle around for five or six hours until she gets home. I guess I could read, write, watch TV, exercise, or take a nap. But Ruki knows I haven't been able to do any of these things. I'm just bogged down by inertia, the lethargy of grief. It has seeped into my cells and tissue and bones and I have no recipe for detox. But *my* grief is *my* job, not something my fifteen-year-old daughter has to feel responsible for. I pat the couch beside me, invite Ruki to sit down.

'I know you're worried about me. I also want you to know I won't be fine, not for a while. But I'll be okay. It's only been three weeks,' I choke here, still unable to finish most sentences without pausing to swallow. 'I love how you want to take care of me, how you want to quit the play to be with me, but I'm not going to let you do that. You have to trust that I'm going to be okay.'

I gather her in my arms and we cry together.

'You know, Ruk, it's okay to cry. We love Paati and we miss her. And I'm not going to hide, every time I cry. I want you to know that it's okay to cry when you feel sad. When we cry together, we're here for each other. There are good times and bad. And we share it all. That's what being family means.'

18

$\mathcal{M}$Y ROUTINE GOES SOMETHING LIKE THIS: I GET UP IN THE morning, see Ruki off, shower and get dressed, drive to work, drive back home, cook dinner, pick up Ruki from school after rehearsal, fake an appetite and fight with the food that sits like a lump in my throat, do the dishes, clean the kitchen, kiss Ruki goodnight, then sit down and cry the tears I've worked so hard to hold in all day. And then, it's time to wake up and start all over again.

Reading, watching *Oprah*, chatting with random strangers at checkout or a front desk, and calling India – none of the small pleasures I earlier indulged in bring me any relief. Calling India and not hearing Amma's cheerful voice cuts to the bone.

Grief feels like utter abandonment. Amma has always been in my world. Now I have to go on, find my way alone, without her.

The images play in my head like a sick movie – Amma's bald head and swollen body, the red plastic bangles on her wrist, the broken middle toe, the turmeric paste on her cheeks, the peach nightie. They loop endlessly in nightmarish hypnotic fashion. I'm sure there's an OFF button somewhere in my head, but I can't seem to find it.

I ache for Maya and Vidu, my fellow travellers on this grief journey. But I also feel distanced from them. Vidu's energies are focused on helping her husband recuperate after a heart surgery. Her days are full and purposeful. Maya is swamped by a whole new set of responsibilities, balancing the demands of caring for Appa with a full-time job.

Mahesh and I talk infrequently. He's mired in his life and I just feel like a big needy cry baby getting in his way when he's got more important things to attend to.

Appa has been acting out with the new nurse. It's not unlike the human body after an organ transplant. Appa resists, despite the best auto-immune suppressants in the form of kind words, softened logic and caring reassurances. On a phone call, Maya tells me the latest drama: he locked himself up in the bedroom and refused to eat breakfast or take his morning pills. The nurse rushed outside the house, then begged and pleaded with him, looking in through his bedroom window. Unable to convince him, she called Maya who had to drop everything at work, dash home to salvage the situation and restore sanity.

Both my sisters have clear, specific goals and in some way I envy their single-minded focus.

Being away from Girish is the hardest of all. There is no place to lay my head and let the sorrow pour out of me. I don't have a friend whose shoulder I can cry on; I don't know any one well enough yet. I have acquaintances within the context of work or my writers' group, but no one who knew my mother. Not in the way of a friend who planned my wedding festivities, knitted a sweater for my baby or held my hand when someone I trusted lied to me. I've left that part of my life behind in India.

Everywhere I turn, there are cruel reminders. Like a mom grieving a child's loss is strangely subjected to miles of strollers, I zero in on daughters visiting their mothers in the retirement community. Simple moments unhinge me: an innocuous mother–daughter hug, a daughter doing her mom's laundry, or driving her to a doctor's appointment. They underscore my loss, and fuel my guilt. I failed Amma at a time when she needed me most.

I count the days, and check them off a mental calendar until Girish's return. It is an unrealistic expectation that he's going to save me from my sorrow, rescue me from the clutches of this desperate grief.

—⟨⟨◦●◦●◦⟩⟩—

The library has always been my favourite destination.

In the Delhi suburb where Girish and I started married life, the library was a hole-in-the-wall space. When we moved to Chennai, I became a member of two libraries: Eloor, a single room that housed racks and racks of books; and, the plush British Council Library with its bright orange furniture and comfy couches.

Days after we moved to a Chicago suburb, I stepped into Schaumburg Township District Library for the first time, and thought I'd stumbled into heaven. My imagination can conjure up pretty amazing stuff, but even I wasn't prepared for anything like this: the cavernous carpeted spaces and books housed in two stories; the adult section and the 'Enchanted Forest' for tots, the music and DVD sections, ESL classrooms, computer labs and a cozy café.

Time stands still when I'm in a library: my fingers caressing the thick spines, smelling the ink and gazing at the tall shelves of books that never fail to remind me: so many books, so little time.

It is daunting that I find no solace between the pages of a book now, something I've always counted on for escape. A book got me through most of life's challenges: when Appa's drunken binge pushed me to the fuzzy edges of sanity; when I started married life in a city without a single friend to call my own; when I missed my siblings; as a new mom doing the diaper marathon; and sitting outside the intensive care unit waiting for a white-coated doctor to show up with an update on Appa.

No book holds my attention now. When you've stared death in the face, trite characters and plots seem trivial. Akin to an alcoholic who gags at the sight of the amber liquid he once thirsted for.

Questions buzz non-stop in my head: Why me? Why her? Why now? Where did she go? Images recur, like a screensaver. One particular image edges the rest out, occupies centre stage: Amma's lifeless body in a turmeric-yellow silk sari, its breath silenced. The image is accompanied by a single thought that plays over and over, a record needle stuck in its groove.

We come into this world with nothing; we leave with nothing.
Amma worked hard her whole life, but left with nothing except the one garment she was wearing.

This truth fills me with despair and dread. And if this *is* the truth, my entire life has been a lie. It mocks all that I've ever believed in: success, ambition, material comforts, basically a life of fulfilment. None of it makes any sense. I feel a void.

You come into the world an innocent infant full of potential and possibility; you grow up and get an education; you get the right degrees; you get a job; you get married; have kids; they grow up and have kids; and if you're lucky, you get to bounce your grandkids on your knee before you die an average unglorified death. Is this all there is?

Something tells me this script is incomplete; that I'm missing a vital link here.

And again, the single tormenting image. Amma's body draped in a yellow sari, the only earthly possession she took with her – that too, only as far as the crematorium.

Where do the pieces fit, I begin to wonder. The struggle to find the perfect job, the one that makes you feel like a million bucks even if it doesn't bring home anything close? The rented apartment which mocks you, so you obsess about finding ways to increase your real estate footprint? The scooter, the car, then the bigger car, the fancier car ... and on and on, this relentless quest for 'stuff' we never get to take, any way.

I wander around the library for hours, the questions growing louder inside my head – just so I don't have to stay home alone and wrestle with them.

Just as I turn to head out, I come to a dead halt in the non-fiction aisle. A book screams out loud at me. A book I've glimpsed many times in the past, and know to be an Oprah's Book Club selection – *A New Earth: Awakening to Your Life's Purpose* by Eckhart Tolle. I don't quite understand the urgency, but I lunge and grab it like it's the last copy on the planet.

When I get home, turn the pages, and start to read, I cannot put it down. It has me hooked like a spy thriller, only it's chockfull of philosophy that's all new to me. Tolle refers to the ego as the false self, and illumines the need to awaken to a new consciousness from the place of one's true self. I drink deep, waking from a long, dry thirst, as if this is the book I've been waiting for, the answer to life's recent anguish.

When you die, the book proclaims, you will be judged on the basis of your true self, and how well you lived your life according to its tenets. Amma's life flashes before my eyes. A+ all the way, I think to myself. She scores big because she had no desire to be right, to win the arguments, to walk over others. For most of my life, I had a word for it: doormat. I watched how she never let petty quarrels upset her rhythm, was rarely offended, and hardly ever blamed any one, no matter what was going on in her life. What I'd always seen as weakness I now begin to know is strength.

Over the weeks, books on death and dying and the afterlife begin to fascinate me. Elisabeth Kübler-Ross's *On Life after Death* explains that Amma shed her cocoon (physical body) and became a butterfly in death. I love the image of Amma as a colourful butterfly, flitting about sunlit gardens, drinking deeply to fill her soul, free and untethered in a way her earthly life could never be.

One evening, I pick up a copy of Sogyal Rinpoche's *The Tibetan Book of Living and Dying* and flip through the pages. A friend handed me the book before I left Chennai. I skip to part two: Dying. The first words in the section speak to me: 'In a hospice I know, Emily, a woman in her late sixties, was dying of breast cancer. Her daughter would visit her everyday and there seemed to be a happy relationship between the two. But when her daughter had left, Emily would nearly always sit alone and cry. After a while it became clear that the reason for this was that her daughter had refused completely to accept the inevitability of her death …'

The words sock me in the solar plexus. It sounds so similar to Amma's story, and mine. A voracious appetite stoked, I read further.

Every page I turn, key concepts jump out at me: compassion, forgiveness, preparing to die, and dying well. Concepts I've never considered, too busy living life. The words make me feel petty and childish. I consider the futility of the energy we invest in hanging on to grudges and offences, real and imagined. The truth: it all evaporates the instant our breath leaves the body.

The sense of urgency I experience is so powerful I stride to my desk, flip open my laptop and make a list of names. They are the people I've wronged and need to make amends with: a dear friend with whom I fell out over a silly argument; a business contact whose actions I'd silently questioned and blamed; a friend whose life I'd disappeared from. Dredging up incidents and names from the hidden recesses of my mind is strangely liberating.

Over the next half an hour, I compose e-mails to each of them, rendering an apology, resolving a conflict, taking ownership, letting go. When I'm done, my moral slate wiped clean for now, I feel a sense of deep peace in the centre of my being. So much better than the bitter acid that churned in my gut making me hold on, grasp, want to be right.

These books are my first encounters with a sliver of peace, a feeling that just, may be, there is meaning to this madness we call the earthly journey. Buried beneath the chaos and ruins of my tragic situation are treasures that I'm slowly waking up to.

19

When Girish returns home on 3 March, the tears I have dammed up in his absence come pouring out of me. He holds me for a long time, my tears soaking into his executive shirt. My husband has always done everything in his power to secure my parents' well-being. This was the one time he couldn't control the end-result.

Over the next weeks, we make an effort to settle into the rhythms of a familiar routine: cooking meals, cleaning, shopping and doing laundry. In performing these tasks day after day, week after week, we hope we can somehow move time along. The further this storm recedes from our lives, the closer to shore we will be, travelling in the direction of safety.

But grief has other ideas. It teases me, trips me up, and tears me apart, just when I'm beginning to believe the worst is over. A word, a smell, a memory, a melody: the intruders lurk at every corner and dart out at me when I least expect them to.

Sometimes, there are no obvious triggers. Laundry has nothing to do with grief. Or so I thought. As I'm scooping the detergent powder into the washer, a swell knocks me over. I struggle to come up for air. I manage to put together a perfectly decent dinner for the family, settle into the armchair for a breather, and a wave of grief crashes over me. Unexpectedly, I'm reduced to a snivelling, sobbing mess.

In an e-mail to Maya, I say: '... there are times when I feel nothing will cure me of Amma's passing. She was almost too good to be true. When I think of her, I cry for the deep sense of loss I've suffered, we've all suffered. I can't imagine going to Chennai and not seeing her, not having long conversations with her, not doing all the things I used to do with her … I cry for Appa and his loss. How difficult this is for him. Will we ever get over losing Amma? There will never be any one like her ever again, and that saddens me terribly.'

Maya, Vidu and I trade daily e-mails, shed virtual tears, give each other cyber hugs. Mahesh seldom calls. On the rare occasion that we talk, he sounds as stunned as I feel. There's always a did-we-really-lose-her element of disbelief that overshadows our conversations. But between shining for corporate America and sharing toddler duties at home, he's distracted, able to move away from the swirling vortex of sadness that I find myself trapped in. I tell myself he's a man, a son. His brain, I imagine, is wired differently to respond to grief and loss. We sisters seem to be speaking a shared language. Yet, he's the only blood relative I have in this part of the world. I count my blessings even if they come in rare minutes of conversation.

My husband, I'm certain, was last in line when God handed out words. In coping with my grief, he's used up the few he had and clearly doesn't know what to say any more.

He gazes at me, bewildered. It's a look that says *I know you're in there somewhere, but I can't find you.* He doesn't know how to reach me. I'm thrashing around in the swirling currents of grief and all he can do is wave a feeble hand and yell over the rush of the waters.

'Haven't you cried enough?' he asks, his voice full of deep sighs.

Speechless, I stare at him.

'You're going to make yourself ill.'

'I don't care,' my voice is sharp, hurt-edged.

'I say this because I care.'

'Don't tell me … how …' I throw my hands in the air, give up.

I somehow have no way to explain why this happens, how little control I have, how I can't make it go away and flick on my happy switch.

For a brief instant, I think back to my American physician's suggestion that I swallow anti-depressants to fake the good feeling. I'd politely declined, in favour of cleansing tears, prayer, and yoga – if I could get my mind to still its chatter for a second. I have never believed in repressing my emotions. It's like trying to shut the door on a messy closet, pretending it doesn't exist and hoping it will be magically restored to order. Until you open the closet door, face what's inside and do the work of cleaning and reordering and tossing and keeping, the mess stays right there, waiting for your readiness to face it. Unlike a closet, the human body creates disease with unresolved feelings, a far more dangerous reality.

A chasm yawns between my husband and I, only a rusty, creaky bridge between us, one neither of us trusts. So we retreat into sullen silences, resentment, and a lack of grace.

The words perch on the tip of my tongue: *How would you know what this feels like?* But I bite them back. It's just another way of saying: *I'm sorry your parents are still around.*

This is the honest truth. Someone who hasn't lost a parent can't come close to knowing what this rawness feels like.

In other ways, Girish has context; I have none. As I'm doing the dinner dishes, Girish knows his parents will be lacing their sneakers back home in Mysore, getting ready for their morning walk. When he tunes into the night news, his father is settling down to a breakfast of oatmeal, buttered toast and a palm full of coloured pills. His mother will be shaking water off a bunch of spinach leaves, ready to chop them and flavour the lentil broth she's making for lunch. Thursday nights, he knows they'll be listening to their favourite music show.

My mother's life is over; my father's, altered forever. How can I expect my husband to understand, to empathize? He hasn't walked in those shoes. Not yet.

20

$\mathcal{O}$VER THE NEXT COUPLE OF MONTHS, WORK GAINS A STEADY momentum. The seventh floor computer lab is up and running.

For a few hours a day, my colleague Andy helps me forget. I feel like the winds of fortune blew Andy into my life, a happy gust of much-needed levity at a time when the thick dark clouds of depression are pressing down on me. His corny jokes, insatiable curiosity about everything Eastern, his antics and wicked sense of humour are all a welcome distraction.

In a matter of weeks, we're best buddies. We make a good team, Andy and I, the perfect complement to each other.

It works to my advantage that Andy has the magic touch when it comes to machines, an area where my brain is missing a few key chips. I still write entire books in long-hand. Probably why I'm the perfect fit in a computer lab for seniors, the only place where I can legitimately strut my stuff. It is such a boon to be able to holler for Andy when photos refuse to upload or I'm desperate to retrieve a lost password.

On the flip side, I'm the one that can spend hours administering a large dose of TLC when seniors travel back in time and tell stories about growing up on a farm, or during the Depression. At the end of the session, both of us are happy. Rich with nostalgia, they shuffle off, but I'm richer for a treasury of cultural literature. Still, through all of this, my personal pain lies just beneath my skin , and on occasion, Andy is witness to it. One day, I couldn't stop the tears running down my face.

Andy looks at me, pauses and speaks up.

'My roommate is a mentor. He works with the Christian youth

group, people who have life challenges and want to grow out of them. May be you should meet him.'

A wall rises inside me. I don't want to go to some Bible-spouting guy who will most likely force me to read scripture verses because I need to be saved. Besides, what do I have to say to someone who didn't even know my mother? I swat the suggestion away.

Unknowingly, a seed has been planted. It lies there, germinating silently.

It is May, three-and-a-half months since Amma's passing.

With Mother's Day around the corner, we plan to promote our memoir project at the retirement community. Enrolling seniors to write their life stories, or tell us their stories so we can help write it for them, is the basic premise. The plan is to cash in on family reunions that happen at the special Mother's Day community brunch.

My idea is to do placemats with a list of questions on a mother's life. Questions like: What was it like, going to school in the 1930s? Where did mom and dad meet for the first time? What was mom's favourite band when she was a teenager? The idea is to get people interested in our memory books, a life story project that mothers and daughters/sons can bond over to preserve a legacy.

I'm excited because I have a fun project to sink my teeth into. Together, Andy and I iron out all the logistics and present the plan to our supervisors who give us the go-ahead.

As Mother's Day draws closer, the butterflies in my stomach start to flap their wings. Is this a good idea? Why did I think going to the community and watching all those mothers and daughters locked in loving embraces, sharing gifts and stories would be easy for me? Do I have it in me to be emotionally resilient at a time like this?

Ironically, Mother's Day is not such a big deal in India, often passing like a ship in the night. In the US, however, the media frenzy is relentless. From television commercials to Hallmark cards, gift baskets, songs on the radio and *Lifetime Movie Network* are milking the moment for all it's worth. Suddenly, everywhere I look there are mothers and daughters: in picture frames, in real life, on my TV screen. I feel orphaned.

Despite my noble intentions, I wish I hadn't committed to the event at The Palms. Now, I have no option but to show up. *What was I thinking?*

It is this feeling that sits heavy on my chest when I wake up on 10 May. Ruki holds me tight. Girish hands me not one, but an entire bunch of cards. When I flip open my laptop, an e-mail from my supervisor Lori cracks me wide open.

'I just wanted to let you know,' she writes 'that I'm sending you positive thoughts and love as you experience a bittersweet Mother's Day. Enjoy the love of the residents and enjoy the memory of your mother. You are amazing – and I'm certain your mother had so much to do with that. You're in my thoughts.'

And then I think of all those mothers and daughters. I think of Amma's life story, the bits and pieces I have, and worse, the bits that are now lost to me forever. I think of all the stories that could be shared, the legacies that will live on. In a moment of acute clarity, I know I can do this. I'm fuelled by a bigger purpose, the possibility of a precious gift to all those mothers and daughters, one that I can help engineer.

When I arrive, the community is abuzz with activity. It is a mom parade, all outfitted in their best finery, powdered and pretty. Adult children, grandchildren and great-grandchildren flock around and fuss over them with gift bags, love and attention.

The atrium is beautifully decorated with fresh flowers and bunting. Tables are set up with crisp white cloth napkins, place mats, silverware – all ready for a delicious connection over food and drink.

As families start to stroll into the building, Andy and I are stationed in the foyer, our publicity materials neatly stacked on a table. Interested folks pause, ask a question or two about our programme, flip through a flyer. We gently persuade them to sign up their moms and/or dads to work with us on their memoirs. Others treat it as an unnecessary distraction in a day which is all about lunch-and-run.

Half an hour later, Andy and I wander into the dining area to encourage adult children to quiz their moms on first dates, fun events and family traditions.

At the first table is a mother stabbing the meat on her plate as if it were a mean ex-husband. Her daughter is staring off into the distance, and occasionally glances at her watch.

I stop at their table, open my mouth to speak. 'No, thanks, we'd just like to eat,' the daughter says, through tight lips.

The mother looks up from her plate. 'Don't you have mothers?' she asks.

Andy and I beat a hasty retreat.

We move to a corner of the room and survey the tables before deciding who would be safe to approach. A giggly, chattering family catches my eye. 'Over there,' I whisper to Andy.

When we get to the table and explain what we're about, a sixty-something man responds with, 'What a neat idea!' Then, he turns to his mother. 'Hey, mom, what do you think? Do you want to tell us about the time you sneaked off with dad on your first date?'

His mom grins across the table. She fiddles with the pearls on her neck. 'Let's see ... that was ...' Brows furrowed, she gives up. 'Oh, never mind,' she waves a hand, a big fat pearl sitting in the middle of a ring on her middle finger. 'I can't remember a thing these days.'

'You know that red dress you hung on to forever?' her son persists. 'That dress had something to do with a date ...'

It is a welcome change, the family at this table. We leave them with a flyer and some information they can go over, happy to have started a conversation heading in the right direction.

Some families take the activity seriously; others fob off our advances with a polite we'd-just-like-to-eat-our-lunch-in-peace-thank-you smile.

If I have adopted a favourite saying, it is this: *When an elder dies, a library burns down.* I repeat it to adult children, those who remain unconvinced about reopening the rich vaults where their parents' stories lie, waiting to be unearthed. For me, it now takes on the nature of a mission I'm committed to, and will continue to aspire to: preserving the stories of their generation.

Doing the rounds, I run into a noisy Italian family: the Rossis. Pamela Rossi, the elderly mom, is the star of the show today. Wearing a pale peach dress and jewellery that prefers to hide, she's revelling in her queen bee status while her family buzzes around her attentively.

One of her daughters, a middle-aged woman, nudges my elbow. It is clear that she has something to say. We break away from the group. As we face each other, I see concern fill her warm, brown eyes.

'She's not always like this,' the woman begins.

I imagine she registers my blank look, for she explains. 'Mom, I mean. We've tried everything, but she just won't get out of her apartment. Stays in there all day, would you believe it?'

I do believe her. She's not the only daughter with a mother who has an isolation issue.

'Is she … unwell, or something?' I ask, needing a little more to go on.

'Oh, no, she's just a hermit.'

'What did she enjoy doing in her younger days? You know, hobbies and stuff. They have a lot of groups here.'

The woman swats a hand and says, 'She won't go to any of those. We've tried, like I said.'

As I begin to wonder why she's imparting this information to me, she introduces herself. 'I'm Lee.' She points in the direction of the family table, adding, 'I'm the second of seven children.'

I introduce myself, wait for more. Waiters bearing silver platters of food weave in and out between tables. Chatter fills the room.

'I was just … wondering … is there something you can do for her? I heard about the computer programme they've introduced here …' Lee trails off.

'Oh. Yeah,' I say without an ounce of conviction in my voice.

Someone who won't leave her room to mingle with real human beings is not going to jump up with excitement at the prospect of learning how to talk to a machine. I don't like that my optimism suddenly plummets to my ankles.

Lee refuses to give up. 'Well, it's worth a try. You said something about a programme on Mondays.'

She's done her homework. She knows the Connect 101 agenda.

'Oh,' I'm suddenly waking up to the implication of what might be feasible. 'Yes, I could try to get her to attend our Monday presentations.'

There's a new confidence in my voice because I know the topics we present are exactly what nostalgia-ridden seniors yearn for: big band music of Glenn Miller and Dizzy Gillespie; *Dorothy and the Wizard of Oz*; Gene Kelly *Singin' in the Rain;* and Clara Bow, the 'It' girl and silent movie star. 'The seniors love travelling back in time, and I'm sure Pamela will find something to enjoy.'

'Oh, good,' Lee says, a glimmer of hope enlivening her eyes. ''Cause you know this kind of isolation is just not good for her. I worry about it.'

'I understand. I'll do something about it,' I promise, without the foggiest idea how to effect a transformation from celebrated cocoonist to social butterfly.

'Why don't we go back to the table and introduce you to her?' Lee says.

Together, we walk over to the table. Pamela shakes my hand tentatively, a slow smile spreading over her face. She doesn't feel like a challenge to me. I feel better about getting her into the fabric of community life.

'Mom, this is Uma. She works here,' Lee explains. 'They have an interesting programme every Monday.'

'We don't have to talk about it now,' I hasten to reassure. 'Can I call you sometime tomorrow?' I venture. The last thing I want to do is tick Pamela off on what is her special day with her family by intruding and blah-blahing my spiel about Connect 101.

Pamela nods, and smiles again.

As I say my goodbyes and saunter away from the Rossi table, I think back to the senior citizens back home in India. Surrounded by a clucking brood of children, grandchildren, nieces, nephews and neighbours, the complaint of loneliness is last on their list. Even as I think the thought, a new one intrudes. That situation is changing, with nuclear family structures and increased urbanization.

21

 ᴀ week later, on Sunday morning, I call Pamela and introduce myself. Thankfully, she remembers me.

I've spent enough time in the community to know this is not a blessing you take lightly. On days, I've waited thirty minutes for a resident to show up for our computer lab appointment, only to realize that she's forgotten all about it. Then I go over to her apartment and knock on the door, but she has no memory of me, let alone setting up a time to work together.

I tell Pamela a little about the presentation scheduled for the following day.

'Why don't you call me again tomorrow morning? Say around half-past nine. I can't seem to remember anything these days,' she says.

This is easier than I'd imagined.

'Sure, I can do that,' I say, making a note in my organizer.

Monday, I call as promised, but Pamela fobs me off. 'I don't feel too well. I'll try for next Monday,' she says.

I hang up, a tad disappointed.

Over the next three Mondays we do the same dance: I call Sunday evening; she requests a Monday reminder call; I call and she makes an excuse.

I decide that a personal visit is in order. It is eleven on a Tuesday morning when I find myself outside apartment 427. I tap lightly on the door. No response. I knock again, fidget as I wait. Nothing. I turn the knob. The door eases open immediately.

I poke my head into the sweetest-smelling apartment in a senior living community. It smells of lavender and rose. 'Pamela ...' I call softly.

No one answers. I step in, shut the door behind me, and take in the room. Everything is pristine and orderly – the furniture dusted and polished, the carpeted expanse of floor spotless, and everything in its place. The couches are upholstered in a pale fabric and patterned with delicate roses.

The bedroom door is closed. I walk towards it and knock gently. This time I hear a thin voice. 'Come in.'

I let myself into an inky black bedroom. The shades are drawn tightly shut. All I can make out is the bare outline of a figure in bed, covers drawn up to the chin, thinning salt-and-pepper hair spread out on the pillow.

Pamela is facing away from me.

I move close to her and whisper, 'Pamela, are you all right?'

'I have the stomach flu,' she says, her voice raspy.

'Did you take something for it?'

'Mmm ... hmm.'

'I just came by, to, you know ... well, you've been feeling unwell a lot, so I thought I'd check in.'

'That's very nice of you. Sit down,' she says, repositioning herself to face me.

I sit in an armchair beside her bed.

'I'm sorry. I've cancelled on you a lot,' she says.

'Don't worry about it.'

'But you don't give up, do you?' she laughs.

Have a lot of people in her life given up on her?

I allow myself a tiny smile. If anything, I'm dogged about getting Pamela out of bed and into the presentation room.

'Don't you want some light in here?' I ask tentatively. If she's determined to cloister herself in here, people-proof herself, a dribble of sunshine wouldn't hurt.

'Oh, I'm sorry,' she says, as if the reality of her dungeon-esque existence never occurred to her, not until I mentioned it.

There's only enough room for the bed, an armchair and a dresser. I edge around her bed, and push aside the heavy drapes.

Bright sunshine barges in, bathes everything in sight. It is only now that the periphery of this woman's existence comes into view. The surface of the dresser is crowded with photo frames. Family pictures of a large brood, all ages and shapes. Off to the side is an aging yellowed photograph of a young Pamela, and a handsome man I presume is her husband. In the photo, her face is relaxed and carefree, smiling into the sun.

'Big family,' she laughs, watching me gaze at the photos.

'Wow. Yeah, you do have a big family.'

'That's all I did. Raised those seven kids.'

Do they look in on her regularly, I wonder, outside of a Hallmark card occasion.

I turn to her, my eyes lingering on her pale, wrinkled face. Her skin looks papery, fragile, like it might crumple if I took her face in my hands.

I retrace my steps, settle back in the armchair. 'How long have you lived here?'

'Too long,' she says, a response that will become familiar to me over time. It is a stock response uttered by seniors who are baffled by the divine logic in emptying out their coffers to live in a fancy mansion, a purposeless life far beyond the years they imagined.

Over the next fifteen minutes we get to know each other a little better. Pamela shares with me her love for poetry. 'I don't read it any more,' she flicks a hand dismissively.

'We could look up some of your favourite poems online,' I dive in, hoping it might be the incentive she needs to get up to the seventh floor.

Her face reflects confusion and then she asks, 'On the computer?'

'Mmm … hmmm.'

'No, no. I'm too old for that sort of thing.' Another excuse I hear a lot.

'You don't have to do a thing you don't want to. Just sit next to me, and I'll pull up any poem you want.'

If there's one trait you need working with seniors, it is bulldog tenacity.

We chat for a while. When I leave, I'm resolute to get Pamela out of her bed and connected with the rest of the world.

22

$\mathcal{I}_N$ THE COMING WEEKS, MY WORK AT THE RETIREMENT community gradually gains momentum. What started out as a slow, tentative trickle into the world of cyberspace grows into a small but steady flow of residents who seem eager for more. Taking advantage of their four free sessions, they explore the world of bits and bytes.

Some enroll for additional sessions, drawn by the need to stay in touch with families scattered far and wide. Some enjoy the companionship of a lab assistant, arguably the lone attentive listener in their lives. There are those who hand me old black-and-white pictures from another world – a world they're nostalgic for – and request me to upload them on their home page. Oftentimes, it is their twenty-first century grandkids' only peek into a vanished world. Unfortunately, a healthy number of seniors still blanch at the very mention of the c-word, swearing off it forever.

In May, Girish and I hire the services of a realtor to scout for a suitable townhome within the geographical confines of Ruki's school district. Our weekends are spent scouring the neighbourhoods, inspecting potential properties, making detailed lists of pros and cons. Some homes are architectural beauties, but fall short of our requirements: an extra bath and a two-car garage. Some are minimalistic in all aspects except when it comes to the sale price. Some others seem a bit too rundown. One or two seem reasonable on all counts, but just don't feel like the right fit.

We're waiting for the right home to present itself, a home that will tug at our heartstrings and whisper, *I'm the one.*

As the weather warms, our apartment building is overrun by Indian parents who got on a twenty-something-hour flight to visit their sons, daughters and grandchildren for three to six months. Visitors from the tropics pay a small fortune in air tickets, so they try and stretch their stay to between eight and twelve weeks.

Back in India, Appa has decided to live with Maya and Guru, so Mahesh's proposed move to India has come to naught. Maya, Guru and Appa have now moved to a new third-floor apartment: compact, self-contained and adequate for their needs.

Appa is on my mind as I look out of the living room window. Hot sunshine and long days are here to stay. I see the elderly enjoying walks with their adult children, grandchildren on bikes or in strollers, balmy sunshine enveloping them in a cozy glow.

My parents will never experience this.

A pang goes through me. The probability of that event was already dim when we moved to Chicago. There was no way Appa could make the arduous journey; and Amma, being his primary caregiver, had deleted the word 'vacation' from her vocabulary many years ago. But in some corner of my heart, I'd nurtured a faint glimmer of hope. Amma would visit us after Appa's time. We would drive her down the American freeways and show her places: parks, museums, libraries, even malls. The possibility existed in some distant future. However, life had other plans.

I turn away from the window before the happy pictures unhinge me, and find some mundane domestic chore to distract myself.

23

*O*VER THE NEXT WEEKS, MY INSPIRED EFFORTS TO GET PAMELA out of bed and apartment 427 have come to naught. We're still performing the same choreography: her initial yes, my reminder call, and her pleading sickness. At some point I come to the realization that this socialization project just isn't going to get off the ground. I need to honour that. But she loves the fact that I'm still trying.

I visit her regularly now. I've progressed from sitting on her armchair to sitting on her bed. Our conversations touch on all subjects: her college days, falling in love, raising seven kids. She gently eases open closed spaces in her heart and shares her regrets, failures, her life's ledger of rights and wrongs.

Every now and then, I give Andy an update on my blossoming friendship with Pamela. His response is a mock shudder.

'What?' I ask, confused.

'I don't know how you do it,' he says. 'Just go into a resident's apartment, climb on her bed, and listen to her stories.'

I laugh, and probe further. 'Why? What's wrong with that?' I'm still murky about his implications.

'I couldn't,' he shrugs. 'I don't know … it's too …' and he gives up, unable to find a word, a container in which to fit a random relationship between two people from different sides of the planet.

I'm doing the paperwork on a resident who just finished her lab session with me.

'I just feel like someone needs to keep trying with her,' I say. 'I mean, I don't know. What if everyone in her life has given up on her, and I did that too? It seems so wrong.'

I stare out of the window, let out a slow breath. 'Even I don't really know why I keep visiting her. I just feel like I need to.'

It's the best I can do. It's all I have to offer at this time.

———<·>·<>·>———

'I feel like I focused too much on being perfect,' Pamela's eyes grow soft as she leans back into a past only she can see. 'Everything needed to be just right. I'd work myself up polishing the furniture, mopping floors, washing windows, baking. The house was spotless. Everyone who walked in the front door said so. But now I wonder,' and her mind wanders away.

I lose her thread, the one that keeps the story together and tug gently, hoping to lure her back.

'You wonder ... about what?'

'Well, you know ... may be I should've been on that floor playing with the kids, telling 'em stories, just being with them.' She sighs a wistful sigh, shakes her head. 'It seems so unimportant now – all that cleaning and polishing.'

I continue to listen. This is a gift, all this wisdom that comes to me from people like Pamela who have twice the life experience I do. It helps me peek through new windows, shows me how I can change my thinking, and therefore, my view of the future.

'May be it takes eighty-some years,' Pamela's voice drags me back to the present. 'And then you figure it out. By then it's too late. The kids are grown and gone. You can't undo any of it.'

'Well, you did the best you could with what you had,' I say. 'Isn't that all we can ever do?'

'I guess. Even so, I have all these thoughts in my head.' She stops talking. Several seconds of silence ensue. 'There's a lot of time to dwell on stuff now.'

She laughs, and then starts to cough.

I fetch her a glass of water. She takes a sip, 'When you don't have a future to look into, your mind keeps travelling to the past.'

That's why you need to get out of here and be with people who will lift your spirits.

'So, are you coming to the Monday meeting? Will I see you there?' I ask, almost by rote, still eager for her to test her social wings.

'Call me.'

'I will.'

At least we have a code, a lingo that binds us together. It has come to define the texture of our friendship; it is the safe framework that holds us together. She knows she won't go. I know she won't go. She knows I know she won't go. It's just her way of saying, *keep coming back.* It's my way of saying *I'll keep coming back.*

24

*T*HE PENDULUM CONTINUES TO SWING BETWEEN GUILT AND grief.

I have trouble shaking off the guilt that I disappeared from Amma's life when she needed me most. For a whole decade before we moved to the US, I lived ten minutes away from her. The irony is inescapable.

The name Randy – Andy's roommate, the one who mentors youth groups at a local church – pops up in my consciousness every once in a while. I just don't know what I'm meant to do with it.

All my life, I've talked my feelings away. Now, for the first time, my landscape feels friendless. And a big part of it has to do with the fact that Amma lacks a context here. Back home, my friends knew her smile, her favourite actor, the softness that crept into her eyes when she talked about her children's early years.

I have a feeling Ruki and Girish avoid the Amma-word for fear that I, and therefore we, will all detonate emotionally. There's a good chance that I will dissolve into floods of tears, a distinctly distasteful proposition for my strong, silent husband. Or I may shut down in a private sulk. And the worst possibility: I may decide to camp down in the dumps and not emerge for a while. When you've been appointed the family custodian of joy and happiness, responsible for manufacturing it for their enjoyment, they don't have the formula to make it of their own accord.

At least with Randy, there's the promise of undivided attention for an hour or so, and the permission to be open. It's beginning to sound like the release I need, the outlet for the waters of grief to flow through and out of me.

I'm not really sure what a spiritual mentor does for his mentees. *Do I need one at all? Am I ready for one? Is Randy the right fit for me?* Strangely enough, a mentor has been on my wish list to God for some time now – ever since I'd started to nibble at some of life's big questions. However, my mental image of the person has never included theology, beads or saffron robes.

May be I do need Randy's help to sort me out and put me back together.

I pick up my cell phone and make the call. It's a short conversation. Randy explains that we need to figure out what exactly I'm looking for, before we determine whether we're a good mentor–mentee fit. We set a date and time to meet and talk things over.

In preparing for the session and working through some of Randy's questions, an important fact has escaped me completely. It's only when I step into the spacious lobby of a neighbourhood church – our meeting place – that it hits me: Today is 18 June, Amma's birthday.

Randy arrives wearing a sunny smile and faded pair of blue jeans, speaking a language my heart instantly responds to. It isn't just grief that's eating me alive; Amma's passing has suddenly unleashed a series of existential dilemmas I'm feverishly seeking answers to.

As I realize what a huge portent this is, Randy seems like a special delivery straight from heaven. It's like Amma is smiling down at me, at us. Something about this feels very right.

Randy's gentle demeanour, the way he draws me out by asking reflective questions, and his calm presence helps me relax. I fill him in on my family background, growing up in India, my relationship with Amma, my spiritual stance, and confess that I'm in a dark, scary place.

An hour later, we hug each other goodbye. When he tells me he needs to pray over the decision to take me on as a mentee – he'll call in a couple of days – I'm desperately hoping his answer will be an unclouded yes.

25

$\mathcal{T}$HE RIGHT TOWNHOME PRESENTS ITSELF TOWARDS THE END of June. We just know it's a good fit for us. Weekend negotiations crystallize into a final agreement. The deal is done. It's a cozy place in Hoffman Estates, a two-bedroom, two-and-a-half bath, two-car garage home. A home where light pours in from all sides, a place we will fill with love.

There's a flurry of paperwork to handle. We need to terminate the lease on our current apartment and complete the paperwork to take possession of our new home. The next few weeks are all about boxes and crates as we sort, keep and discard. Our books that arrived from India have been sitting in storage for a year, and the prospect of having a home library once again is exciting. For Ruki and me, there's no happier sight than rows upon rows of colourful spines on shelves.

Packing and moving, we miss the conveniences India offers. All our moves in India involved four or five well-muscled men packing our stuff into boxes and crates, loading them on a truck, unloading at our new destination and setting up the dressers, beds, sofa sets and dining furniture where they needed to go. The best part was that this entire operation did not mean our wallet was stretched.

Here, we pack, we stuff boxes, we tape and we move. Only the big-ticket items like our furniture and appliances go on a truck driven by a friendly handyman (introduced to us by our realtor) and ably assisted by his son and son's buddy.

In India, every new venture, no matter its nature – a wedding, buying a new car or a home, a change of employment – is usually preceded by a puja ceremony to invoke the blessings of Lord Ganesha, the god of new beginnings.

The first thing we do after moving into a new home is boil a container of fresh milk on the stove. Then, coffee is made and served to all – sugary and milky, Indian-style.

Girish and I set up a small altar in our home. It is a twenty-first century secular altar in which a gamut of gods resides: from Mother Mary and a bleeding Jesus on the cross to Krishna, Ganesha and Lakshmi, Amma's glasses, my grandfather's photo, and a framed serenity prayer which has been a family favourite since Appa's alcoholism days.

After the milk-boiling ritual, Ruki, Girish and I hold hands and recite the serenity prayer followed by a blessing for our new home. All of a sudden, a wave of homesickness washes over me. Amma had always been present during this ritual at every new home we'd moved into. Her absence today feels significant.

'If there's any place Amma is right now,' Girish says, 'it's right here. She's here in a way she couldn't have been, if she were in Chennai.'

His words ring so true. I shut my eyes tight, try to feel her presence and send a prayer her way. *Watch over us, Amma. Help us make this a happy home.*

That night, I have a dream. In it, Amma walks through the front door and down the length of the hallway towards the living room. The dream is so real that when I awaken I half-expect to find her in the kitchen, making coffee.

I get it, Amma. I know you're telling me you're here with all of us.

That dream sets my mind at rest, makes me hang on to the words my husband offered me with a new clarity.

26

$\mathcal{I}$ TAKE TIME OFF FROM WORK TO MOVE, SETTLE IN AND GET organized. As a result, I spend only an hour or two at The Palms to attend to urgent matters: scheduling computer lab appointments, making follow-up calls to residents, completing paperwork. Then, I rush home and dive into boxes, stuff that needs unpacking, sorting and putting away. A zillion tasks clamour for my attention.

Given my crazy schedule, two weeks go by before I'm able to visit Pamela. That I haven't seen her gnaws at me like a dull toothache I've tried to ignore.

Monday morning I swing by Pamela's apartment, bursting with news of our move. I'm eager to share with her how spacious a townhome feels when you've learnt to squeeze yourself and your possessions into an itty bitty apartment; how nice it is to have a patio with furniture; how convenient it is to simply walk down the stairs and start a laundry load, instead of waiting for a common laundry room washer-dryer to empty.

I push open the apartment door which is never locked.

Something doesn't seem right. I see wires snaking under and into Pamela's bedroom. As I'm trying to make sense of it, I'm startled by a voice. A heavyset black woman gets up off the couch and lumbers towards me saying, 'Can I help you?'

'Yes … I'm Uma. I came by to visit Pamela. And you are … ?'

'Adele. I'm Pamela's caregiver.'

I stare at the woman with the large head, Afro curls and chunky jewellery. Pamela's caregiver!? Pamela had no caregiver the last time I was here. Who's this Adele? And what is she doing here? I'm surprised by the sudden spurt of hot jealousy, the sense of possessiveness that comes over me. Like Pamela's more mine than Adele's.

'May I …' I gesture towards Pamela's bedroom.

'Lemme check and see if she's awake,' Adele stalls me.

I've gone in when she was asleep and you were not even here. She wakes up as soon as she hears my voice.

I wait, seething, while Adele calls out to Pamela, says a lady by the name of 'Yuma' is here to see her. Her mispronouncing my name grates on my nerves. I hear Pamela's guttural voice, although I can't make out the words.

'You can go in,' Adele waves a plump hand, a flamboyant ring on every finger.

Gingerly, I enter Pamela's bedroom. The first thing I notice is the mask obscuring most of Pamela's face. Something catches in my throat as my eyes take in the oxygen cylinder sitting next to her bed.

'Hi,' my voice is weak. 'What happened?'

'I have cancer.' Pamela drops the words in a dull, flat voice.

I have a cold. I have a headache. I have a cut finger.

I have cancer.

Something crushes my chest, my throat, my lungs. I'm desperate for air. A long moment of silence hangs between us.

Rain pelts the window, the sound of someone scattering tiny pebbles on glass.

How did this happen? When did it happen? I saw you only two weeks ago. You were fine. I turn my back and you do this to me.

A chilling realization grabs hold of me. I turn away, and a cancer diagnosis slams my world. This is exactly what happened with Amma.

My limbs turn to liquid. My legs won't support me a moment longer.

'I need to go,' my words rush out. Without waiting for Pamela's response, without saying goodbye, I run out of the room and down the length of the hallway over to the other side of the building, open the door that leads to the stairs and slump down. My body is shuddering with the effort to contain the sobs clawing their way up my throat. My breath comes in quick, shallow gasps. I drop my head into my hands and let the tears come. It's fresh betrayal. A grand lesson I need to be taught repeatedly, because I'm apparently too dense to get the message.

My cell phone rings, shattering the moment. Through my streaming eyes, I see 'Andy' light up on the screen. I ignore the call. Someone must be looking for me. Do I have a lab appointment? I can hardly remember. May be Andy has to call on a resident with a malfunctioning laptop and needs me to man the lab. Whatever it is, it can wait. I'm so defeated I don't care any more.

I'm not sure how long I sit there, staring through a window at the slate-grey sky weeping copiously, just like me. Eventually I gulp a few deep breaths, wipe my face and rise to my feet. As tempting as it is, I can't hide all day. I decide to take the stairs, three floors to the lab. It'll give me time to compose myself and gather my thoughts.

When I walk into the lab, Andy is busy printing documents.

'Where were you?' he asks, pushing a button on the printer. 'Julia waited, like, fifteen minutes. I tried to call you.'

When I don't respond, he turns around to face me. 'Hey, what's up? You okay?'

My red eyes are a dead giveaway.

'Yeah, I'll be fine,' I reply, walking to the large window that overlooks the parking lot. Row after row of cars are parked between parallel yellow lines, a calming picture of orderliness.

'You sure?' Andy persists.

'Pamela has cancer.'

'Oh, man.' He pauses, as if looking for the right words. 'She just found out?'

'I didn't ask. I went by her apartment after two weeks.' Even I hear the frustration in my voice. As if I believe that Pamela wouldn't have been snared by cancer if only I'd been vigilant and visited faithfully.

'It's not your fault. Okay?' Andy tries to bring perspective into my swiftly unravelling life.

I shrug unconvinced, confusion and anger sweeping through me. Cancer snuck in on her because I didn't play my role of guardian angel well enough. The rational part of my brain allows itself a quiet snigger and scoffs at this line of thinking, but my guilt-ridden gut buys into it.

27

My FIRST FEW SESSIONS WITH RANDY, ALL I CAN DO IS CRY. He seems like a safe, non-judgmental harbour to take my storms to. He listens intently while I blubber through my grief. I tell him stories about my life in India, my Amma stories, my falling out of love and break-up with God, and how we're in the making-up phase. All he does is, offer me a vast space for all my stuff to spew out.

Very gently, he guides me away from my relentless quest and futile grasp of 'why'. When he senses my readiness, he opens a tiny doorway. 'One of the things I'd like you to explore is, to ask. Ask yourself *what* you're meant to learn from this, instead of *why* it happened.'

May be he was wrong about my readiness, because I want to jump all over him about this preposterous suggestion.

What do you mean what I'm meant to learn from this? How does one learn from something so horrible? You want to know what I've learnt? I've learnt how painful the feeling of a severed limb is. You don't 'learn' when you lose someone you love so much. A part of you dies with them.

I imagine my internal struggle is playing out on my face, for I can tell Randy knows exactly what I'm thinking, even if the words are invisible. But there is a part of me that reluctantly acknowledges that this man is not trying to be insensitive. He's trying to hand me an oar so I can navigate the choppy waters of grief. Randy is a man of few words and infinite patience. 'Think about it,' he says, as I shrug my coat on and prepare to leave.

28

$\mathcal{F}$OR SOME TIME NOW, NEWS OF MY FRIENDSHIP WITH PAMELA has travelled swiftly on the grapevine. Honestly, I don't see what the fuss is all about. But the fact that I visit a lonely old woman and am determined to socialize her is fresh fodder in a building where people hunger for something, anything to juice up their hollow lives.

So, when I receive a call from a senior staff member from the Dallas head office, I'm more than a little surprised. Concerned about my emotional needs, Marla asks if I want to keep visiting Pamela, given her dire diagnosis. Obviously, this has reached her too. Marla handles the conversation so competently that I'm impressed at the company's sensitivity to employee welfare.

'I see no reason to stop visiting,' I respond. 'I mean, why would I— ?'

'—No, don't get me wrong,' Marla hastens to assure me. 'I know how difficult a time this is for you. With your mother's loss. So ... I was just wondering ...' As I'm considering a suitable response, she asks, 'Anyway, how're you doing with Pamela's diagnosis?'

'It's not easy.'

'I hear you. And although I'm happy you're reaching out to her, you need to take care of yourself too. This is the downside of the job – we all know that even as we fall in love with these seniors and give them a piece of our heart, these are people whose time is running out.'

Over the next few minutes, she lets me in on a personal story, her friendship with ninety-three-year-old Beth. It is the story of an impromptu encounter that connected two hearts in the most meaningful way. Marla tells me of the candid conversations she and Beth shared. No topic was off-limits. For Beth, the friendship with someone who neither knew, nor cared, about her history and her flawed life riddled with mistakes, was immensely liberating. To Marla, it was a bond that shone light on some of the issues she hadn't made peace with for most of her life.

'Beth passed on a year after I met her,' Marla says softly. 'I locked myself up in my room for forty-eight hours. I didn't want to eat or sleep or shower. I mourned that little old lady who'd stolen my heart. And yet, my life had grown so much richer for the friendship we shared.' There's silence on the line, then she talks some more. 'So, believe me. I really know what you're going through. And I want you to also know that you can pick up the phone and call me anytime. Cherish Pamela now more than ever. You have no idea what a gift you are to her.'

Marla's words bring a lump to my throat. Here's an important lesson: It's not blood that connects you to a human being; it's the bridge you build, one heart to another.

⸺⟨⟩⸺

Now that Adele is in charge, Pamela's apartment door is always locked. It's Adele who lets me in when I visit these days.

Every time I call on Pamela, it feels like a personal encounter with the most menacing demon living inside my head. I know that very same demon devoured Amma and devastated me. Now, it is Pamela who's under attack. Fear is a monster you can lock away in a closet, but you can never throw the key away. Someday, I'll have to creep back up to that closet. Terror coursing through my blood, I'll have to fling those doors open and look that monster in the eye.

Every time I step into Pamela's apartment, I have no idea what to expect.

Today, a whiff of cigarette smoke hits me the moment I enter. Adele has caught the frown on my face, for she says, 'She's havin' a smoke, In the bathroom.'

'She smokes!?'

'Yeah, that's why the lung cancer.'

I had no clue. How would I? Pamela is always in bed when I visit. May be she waits for me to leave and then lights up. I know smoking inside the building is against the rules, but I've known more than a few residents who bend, stretch or just openly flout the rule.

'But now!? With the cancer?' I struggle to keep the incredulity out of my voice.

I think of how Amma followed every rule in the book – watching her diet, taking her medicines on time, and getting enough rest after chemo sessions – to give her body a fighting chance.

'Well, now she say it make no difference,' Adele explains. 'Her kids say it's okay, let her be.'

She's given up.

In some corner of my heart, I'd known all along. That's why she drew the drapes, got under the covers, and stayed there.

Five minutes later Pamela emerges, the strong smell of nicotine pervading the entire apartment. Adele helps her into bed, tucks the bedcovers around her, and shuts the door behind us as she leaves. Pamela's face is tired, drawn.

'How're you feeling today?' I ask.

'I'm doing okay.' Okay, I now know, means 'not too good.'

I sit on her bed and reach for her hand. It's icy cold.

'Pamela,' I begin. 'Can I ask you something?'

'Sure.'

'Are you scared?' I ask.

'Scared?' she thinks for a moment. 'You mean, scared of dying?'

I nod.

'A little, I guess.'

When you're not a daughter or a niece or a sister-in-law, there is a certain freedom to cross over to emotional territory that is otherwise forbidden to close family. I just posed a question to

Pamela that I never could have with Amma. And she responded with as much honesty and clarity as she could muster.

'What's it like outside?' she asks.

'The weather, you mean?'

'Mmm … hmm.'

'It's a seventies day.* Bright. Not too windy,' I leave out the powder-blue sky, the sunshine that's pouring over everything, and the tender green of miles of grass.

She sighs. In her long regretful sigh, I hear the pain of being denied the simple pleasures of golden sunshine and clouds in the sky.

'I'm done here,' she says, after a brief pause. 'There's nothing to live for.'

My throat is tight. 'Oh, Pamela. You can't give up. What about your family?'

'Oh, they have lives of their own. I'll just be one less thing to take care of.'

I think back to my childhood when Thaathi, Appa's mother, was as much a part of the family as Amma, Appa and us, four siblings. I think of Paati, Amma's mother, who at ninety-two still lives with my uncle, aunt and nephew. She's been witness to her grandson's every rite of passage: from a chubby-cheeked toddler to wild adolescent to the strapping young man he is today.

I dearly wish Pamela had such a protective cocoon, especially at a time like this. However, I'm beginning to understand the push-pull dynamics of the senior care trend in this culture. Seniors blanch at the very idea of sharing space with their adult children; and equally, the offspring fail to comprehend how they could all live under the same roof without someone killing the other.

Much as I want to stay with Pamela, I know I should go. It's time for my next appointment. Walter is a stickler for punctuality. I have no desire to be subjected to a lecture about the present generation's complete disregard for clocks and calendars.

*Refers to 70 degrees Fahrenheit, which indicates a pleasant weather.

'I'll come see you tomorrow,' I say, planting a kiss on Pamela's dry cheek. I hold her hand a moment longer, unwilling to let go. My breath catches in my chest. Every time I leave her apartment, I'm not sure there will be a tomorrow for her, for us.

———<⊙•⊙•⊙>———

Pamela spends the last few days of her life in a hospital, and never returns to her apartment that smells of lavender and roses. It is a bright August afternoon, the day she passes on.

I hide in the stairwell and cry my eyes out. Then I pull out my cell phone, call Marla and cry some more.

'Take heart, Uma,' she consoles. 'You were the joy in Pamela's life. You brought meaning into it, in whatever way she was able to receive it. May be she didn't have the words to tell you how she felt about you, but don't ever doubt that she felt it.'

She goes on to explain how those we lose never lose us. They see us, hear us and continue to share in our joys and sorrows.

In the afternoon, I am in no shape for any work that demands even a modicum of intelligence so I reschedule my appointments and bury myself in numbing paperwork. An hour later, as I start to put files away and clear my desk, Dave, the executive director of the building, makes an appearance. He takes my hand, and simply says, 'I'd like you to come with me.'

As we ride the elevator and navigate the corridors, panic claws its way up my throat. We're headed to Pamela's apartment. Suddenly, my brain is flooding. *Is she in there? Where's Adele? What am I supposed to do here? Are they going to have me identify something?*

And just like that we're standing outside her apartment and I'm shaking. Dave grips my hand tight as if to say '*It's going to be okay*'. He pushes the door open, and there's a room full of people.

'This is Uma,' he tells them.

There is a flurry of motion, and I find myself being hugged over and over again. All seven of Pamela's daughters and sons and a few of their spouses are here. Some of them are red-eyed; others look composed. I know from experience that this is probably the calm before the crazy grief.

All I want to do is flee. This is overwhelming, standing in a room full of Pamela's family, and no Pamela.

Names rush at me as they tell me who they are.

Questions fly from all sides:

'What did you two talk about?'

'Did Mom say anything about me?'

'Was she scared to go?'

'Did she whine and complain about us?' This is followed by an awkward laugh.

I feel trapped. I don't know how much to say, how much to hold back. Our conversations – Pamela's and mine – were ours alone, something to treasure. So I walk the tightrope, giving them enough to satisfy their curiosity without compromising Pamela's confidences. Knowing how significant the moment is, I dwell on how Pamela wished she'd been a better mother, and they all go 'Aww'.

'She went peacefully,' one of her daughters informs me.

'Yeah. We're relieved she's not suffering any more,' her husband adds.

Then Lee comes forward and gives me a hug. She's the one who connected Pamela and me on Mother's Day, the spark that lit a beautiful friendship. 'Thanks for everything you did. She always talked about you. Told us how beautiful Indian women are.'

I offer a sad smile. They all look at me, as if I'm expected to deliver a speech at this point. Fortunately for me, Dave saves the moment.

'Pamela never did get out of the apartment, but Uma wormed her way in,' he says, then looks at me as if to say: *I just delivered your opening line.*

'Well,' I begin, 'I'm just happy I got to know Pamela. I got more out of our friendship, that's for sure. She was such a kind, loving soul. Wherever she is right now, she knows I love her.'

They all crowd around me in a flurry of thank yous. A little later, Dave and I leave the apartment.

In befriending this woman, I know I opened up my heart space and let the pain of her cancer march right into my woundedness. Could I have done it any differently? I'm not sure. I turn my face heavenwards.

Amma, I couldn't be there for you, but I could be here for Pamela.

We don't always get to choose who we serve and how. I was moved continents away from Amma, but I was also placed in Pamela's path.

29

WHERE IS AMMA?

The question is like a mosquito, the annoying buzz in my ear. Is she in the air around me? In the big leafy tree outside my window? The clouds? The big blue yonder?

No matter where I was, I'd always known where Amma was. In my mind, she always had a physical context: stirring a fragrant pot of rasam on the stove; folding undershirts and towels as she watched a favourite soap; standing next to Appa's bed and cooling a davara of milk; on the front porch chatting with aunty-next-door.

Over the years, as jobs and then married life took me away from home, it has always comforted me, this knowing. When I missed her, I placed her in her physical context and thought of what she might be doing. Not so hard to do, considering that my mother's was a limited universe, mostly confined to the four walls of the home. She mostly stuck to a set routine. If there was something out of the ordinary, like a doctor's appointment or a visit to Paati's, we all knew in advance. Ever since Appa's accident in 1994, such an outing has required careful planning and coordination.

Now she feels lost to me. Her physical absence is so real, even across the thousands of miles. The absence of her voice on the phone every time I call Chennai is a painful reminder. Oftentimes, I feel like a branch cut off a tree, severed from family news and happenings. My source is gone, the stories have dried up.

When I think of Amma now, there is a vacuum.

I keep searching, in waking moments, in my dreams. She feels utterly real when she slips into my mind space at night, but the moment I wake up, she disappears with the dream. In the milky light of dawn, I hold tight to the tendrils of that dream, stretch it a little longer, try to make it last. I am a kindergartner all over again clutching a tiny fistful of my mother's sari, unwilling to let go.

⸺ ❮ ❀❀ ❯ ⸺

Those familiar with bereavement say the firsts are the hardest to get through.

The first significant hurdle in my path is my forty-fifth birthday. Unlike other birthdays when times were more normal, the sense of anticipation surrounding the day is definitely missing.

When I awaken that morning, my first thought is of Amma, the person who gave me the gift of life. I'm here because of her, and she's here no more. I close my eyes and stay in bed.

The Girishes have a tradition. The two whose birthday it is not, get out of bed and wake up the person whose birthday it is, by singing the Happy Birthday song. Sure enough, moments later, the two voices I love the most harmonize. What is missing is the usual joy with which I've greeted the dawn of my birthday.

I offer up a thin smile, the covers pulled up to my chin. They peel the covers off, hold me by the hand, help me out of bed and wrap their arms around me. Next, they lead me to the den, and to my gift-wrapped presents and cards. I open the cards, one by one, and linger on the sentiments.

This is a family tradition too: buying multiple cards, instead of just one. Girish picks his cards with care, a mix of humour and intimacy. Ruki's cards are mushy, gushy and lovely. I smile and pick up the first gift. I tug at the sellotape strips gently. What starts out with the noblest of intentions – to preserve the beautiful wrapper and reuse it – is soon lost to a frenzy of impatience. Soon, swiftly shredded wrapper bits lie at my feet.

I gasp. It is a beautiful picture frame with a smiling Amma inside it.

Tears well up in my eyes. Ruki holds my hand, while Girish

says, 'See, she didn't forget the day.'

Exactly my thought.

Amma showed up in her inimitable way and wished me a happy birthday with her wonderful smile, first thing in the morning. Somehow, this doesn't feel like a coincidence. From that moment, her picture occupies a special corner on my writing desk. She's the first person I see when I start my day: penciling my to-do lists, checking e-mail and writing my day's pages. I talk to her, tell her how I'm feeling, ask for guidance.

It's a reassuring reminder. Amma will always be part of my life, guiding and inspiring me from another realm.

—◁◦◦◦▷—

Ruki is ready to start her junior year of high school. Girish, who is responsible for the trade lane logistics between India and the US, is either on the road or in the air and juggling several balls and trying to keep them all from falling.

When we talk, it's about school supplies, gas prices, and even Appa's care. But the familiar well-loved two-syllable word – Amma – is all but forgotten. It's forgotten because she's not on anyone's to-do list any more, and we must get on with the business of living.

Randy steps in to fill this space for me. With him, there are no agendas, no shouldn'ts and couldn'ts, no walls I must erect to keep me and others safe. We select specific books, read chapters from those books and relate the learning to my personal growth challenges.

One of the exercises Randy has me do is write Amma a letter addressing all the unfinished business of our lives as I see it. Amma never, ever took sides where her four children were concerned, but I didn't always understand it. When my brother cut us out of his life, she continued to stay in touch with him, sending him birthday and wedding anniversary cards and updating him on all our news when he called. It angered me that she did; it felt like a betrayal of sorts. I wanted her to choose me and my sisters.

I never did get to tell her that I forgave her, that I see differently now. I doubt I could've chosen between my children, if I'd had more than one.

I pour my heart out in my letter to Amma, say all the things I have had to lock away. When I'm done, I read the letter out loud to her, as if she were in the room. My cheeks are wet with my tears, a healing, cleansing experience.

Amma knew I needed this healing; that's why she sent Randy to me. But my visits with Randy are once a month and last ninety minutes. I always have more to say at the end of that time. So he suggests a 'Grief Support Group' at a local church. Wasting no time, I Google the group and register for the fall session.

September seems a lifetime away, but a group of fellow-bereaved is the closest I'll have to a family here.

30

On A New Earth, Eckhart Tolle's central message is that the present moment contains all of one's power. This power, he advocates, is found in meditation, the practice of centering oneself.

Having read the book from cover to cover, and lured by the promised peace and calm, I decide to give meditation a go.

I wake up early in the morning, find a quiet spot and settle down in cross-legged lotus position, my eyes closed. Having done years of yoga, I know that as you contort your body into challenging positions, the focus is on the muscles as well as the breath.

In meditation, however, there is all the room in the world for my mind to wander.

Deep breath in, belly fills up like a balloon. Slow exhale, belly collapses.

Did Ruki remember to take her lunch bag?

Deep breath in.

My armpit is itching.

Hold for three counts.

Must remember to renew those library books or there'll be a fine to pay.

Exhale, whoosh.

Must Girish have such a noisy shower? Sounds like a waterfall in there.

I crack my eyes open, steal a glance at the clock.

Forty seconds!?

I'll never be any good at this. This stuff is for sages and sadhus who sit in the stillness of the Himalayas. Not real people like me who live in a Chicago suburb and struggle to find silence in the midst of the jerky roar of a lawn mower.

Focus, concentrate, come back to your breath.

Within three seconds, my mind floats away like a helium balloon, its chatter growing worse.

You're a loser. You can't even sit still for ten minutes. Who do you think you are? Some enlightened being sitting under a bodhi tree? Get real. Go make some buttered toast and strong coffee.

Even I don't know how I manage to go through the charade of meditating for ten minutes. What is supposed to make you centred and energized has me feeling frazzled and like a failure. I beat myself up for not having attained some elusive standard of peace. But I'm determined to come back and give it another try tomorrow morning.

With all the noise inside my head, I can barely hear myself. To be able to listen to the part of me that knows, the part that is my soul, I need to get really quiet. At least, this much I know: I'm a seeker. Of silence.

31

*U*NLIKE HAPPINESS OR EVEN FEAR, THE GRIEF OF LOSING A loved one cannot be shared with someone who hasn't known it: the sudden pressure in the middle of the chest; the fog of fatigue that blankets you without warning; the panic that grips you by the throat and screams that you can never go back to life as it used to be.

I haven't the faintest idea what a Grief Support Group will do for me, but somewhere inside of me is a resonant *ping*. It's a group that meets weekly for two hours, over nine weeks.

My mind conjures up a picture: a club of mourners all clad in funeral black, wearing expressions of devastation. A group I will fit right into.

Getting ready for my first meeting, I feel buoyant. Like a shipwreck survivor who has just spotted the rescue squad. There's the flip side as well: doubt, trepidation. *Is this the magic cure that will make my grief go away?*

What I imagine to be a spartan church setting looks more like a fancy spa than a place of worship. Conditioned by the austerity of a temple, I am instantly goggle-eyed at the interiors: the cool curtain of water and endless lobby area, the café stocked with cookies and colourful cakes, the library, and the sheer steel-and-glass structure that is Jesus's home. Wall posters of scripture verses and computer stations lend the foyer a sophisticated aura. It is a world away from the rough-hewn stone walls and fading paint of ancient Indian temples. Later, I learn that this is a non-denominational church, one that welcomes people of diverse faiths. A comforting thought.

The grief group meets in a large auditorium. I stand in the doorway for a moment and take it all in: the circular tables, eight to ten chairs, placards with table numbers and category of grief support. People are wandering about with dazed expressions. Around the room are tables propped with category-of-grief placards: *Loss of Child, Loss of Spouse, Loss of Sibling* and *Loss of Parent*. It's like a survivor camp here, the room heaving with heavy hearts. Amidst the confusion, despair and sadness, I cannot help but be impressed by this organized approach to the processing of a universal emotion. And it's free, this church-run ministry. I scan the room for my table and spot it.

Tamara leads our group, an all-women table. She has soft, kind eyes – the sort that looks right into your soul – and the voice of a slow-winding brook. Now in her thirties, Tamara was a teenager when she lost her mother and journeyed through a period of turbulence when her dad remarried.

A couple of women in my group are grieving the loss of a father; the majority has lost a mother.

Over the next two hours, we hold space for each other. We offer our ears and shoulders and hearts. We weep and yearn and reminisce and revisit. Our Indian, American, German and Swedish skins fall away as we connect the threads of our stories. Grief is a great leveller. Our accents may be different, but our hearts beat as one, our cells look the same. We're all daughters who have lost a parent. We find a common enemy – cancer: throat, lung, breast, ovarian, stomach or brain, it matters not. What does matter is what's left behind – the broken pieces that we're trying to hold together.

We share in a way we've rarely shared before. Last words, significant conversations, words unspoken and those hurled in anger, fears and lost identities. All those things that have brought us here, to this moment, to this table, to each other.

It's nine already. When I get up and give the girls a round of hugs before leaving, I finally begin to glimpse the meaning of the phrase *we are all connected*. It is a timely lesson in universal oneness: when you lose a loved one, you ache because you're human.

Over the following nine weeks, my grief group becomes my inner circle. These women of varied experience open their fragile hearts as they search for a clue, an answer, anything to make sense of the pain. My tears are safe here, free to flow. We pass boxes of tissues when we're together, and connect via e-mail when we're apart. We support, and pray for each other, hold each other through the 'fragile firsts'. There is community in grief, and I feel fortunate to have found it.

Lessons open up for me. Through forty-five-year-old Patty's story I learn that you can't simply shut the door on grief and make it go away. It continues to live in your knees and liver and chest, reminding you that it needs attention.

Saddled with the responsibility of raising six-year-old twin girls as a single mom, Patty shoved the grief of losing her mom into the farthest closet of her mind and got on with the business of living. Twenty years later, the tears dammed up from that devastating loss come rushing out of her. I watch Patty mourn her mom, as if she'd lost her a week ago.

32

$\mathcal{I}$F I HAD TO PICK ONE WORD THAT DEFINES THE THEME OF MY life, it would have to be story. I was born a storyteller. At the age of three, I could recite entire episodes from the Ramayana with such flair Amma used to tell me, that our neighbours were locked in fierce competition for babysitting privileges. As a little girl, I waved my hands and talked to an imaginary audience regaling them with stories and jokes. I started to write stories well before my teen years. When I moved to Chicago, I was well-published at age forty-four.

One of the reasons I love my job at the retirement community is because it revolves around story: sharing, collecting and writing stories. My favourite part of this role is helping seniors record their memoirs on their home page of the community website. I've been treated to a veritable feast of stories: Chicago's famous blizzard of 1967, Grammy's matchless potato pancakes, becoming a nun, a well-loved car sold on the sly by a well-meaning son, running away from home, a first date on a tram and many others.

It occurs to me, these stories are so priceless they need not just a bigger platform, but a safe space. So I come up with an idea for a 'Reminiscences Club' that meets for an hour every week. This is more of a discussion group, not a writing class, which eliminates the barriers of arthritic fingers, shaky hands, and macular degeneration.

Every week, we meet, my group of eight and I. At the end of that one hour, they take away a questionnaire I've prepared for next week's session. Topics include 'Places I've travelled to'; 'My family and faith'; 'Pets'; and 'Growing up during the Depression'.

Occasionally, I vary the menu with a life lesson topic: fear, loneliness, anger, forgiveness and gratitude.

When, three months later, the same seniors keep returning to the group, I know they find value in it. New residents check us out. There are some drifters, some curiosity-seekers, but my core group remains faithful. For those sixty minutes, they trawl through the cobwebby attics of their mind, often stumbling upon forgotten treasures. In reliving the memories, those that make them chuckle in fond remembrance and those that choke their throats, they find release. It can finally be let go. One woman picks up the phone and calls a son she hasn't spoken to in years. Another writes a letter of forgiveness. A third vents her anger on page and burns it, a liberating release ritual.

At Thanksgiving I invite them to write 'gratitude letters' to the unsung heroes in the community: the cleaning crew, the servers in the dining hall, the bus driver and the medical assistants. Slowly they begin to see the point of it all. It is in being expansive and focusing on what's going right in their lives that the doorway to goodness swings wide open. When the time comes for their curtain call, there will, hopefully, be no unfinished business. It will be time to leave in peace.

33

ARTHRITIC FINGERS MANOEUVERING HER WHEELCHAIR, she pushes herself slowly. There's a bright red journal in her lap.

It is noon on a Monday. She stops in front of me, hands me the journal. 'Read this,' she orders. Just like that, with no preamble.

I stare at her, this silver-haired woman dressed in brown slacks and a flowered blouse who looks to be in her seventies. Her eyes are sad and empty. A strong smell of urine floats around her. My nostrils flinch. No matter how long you work with seniors, there never comes a time when you get used to the smell of urine.

I know her face; I've lost her name.

I start to open the journal when her sharp voice cuts in. 'Not here. Take it home. Read it and bring it back to me.'

I can't remember her name.

'What's in it?' I ask.

'My sister wrote it. Read it.' Again, it's not a request; it's a command.

I recall her name.

'I won't be in tomorrow, Marilyn. Can I bring this back to you on Wednesday?'

I have learnt how critical it is to make and keep specific agreements. To a senior, a journal or a photograph is pure treasure. If they're handing it to you, it wouldn't be presumptuous to assume they trust you with their life. Rarely will a senior remember what she ate for breakfast, but she *will* remember the exact moment in time and space when she handed you her precious journal. I must honour that trust.

'Okay. But be sure to read it,' she says, getting ready to roll away.

Now I'm really curious about the contents of this journal.

That night after dinner, I open the journal. The writing is an illegible scrawl. Words are misspelt and the grammar is second-grade level. It is a long letter from Marilyn's sister.

Her sister explains, in broken language, what she knows of their parents, scattered bits of information gathered from an assortment of family members. Not all of it is clear to me, but the gist is a story of neglect. As a result, the parents lost custody of their children. The four kids were divvied up amongst orphanages. As adults, they managed to find each other, but the reality of growing up in different environments has taken its toll. Relationships are in disarray, the brothers preferring the anonymity of disconnection to the unpleasant reminders of a traumatic childhood. I sense the sadness the sisters experienced in this rejection, all over again, this time by their own brothers.

It gives me a lot to think about. My siblings and I grew up with two parents who were far from perfect. But they were there, flawed and frustrating, and doing the best they could to keep us all together. In the light of what I have just read, my parents sprout angel wings and a halo. A shift in perspective is everything in life.

On Wednesday, I find Marilyn in the game room.

'Let's go to the living room,' she whispers, conspiratorially.

When we're settled, she fixes her eyes on me. 'Did you read it?' she hisses.

I nod.

She looks at me, waiting for more.

I look at her, at the painting on the wall, at the floor and back at her. 'It was … what can I say?'

'That's my story. I grew up in an orphanage,' her voice has softened.

I can't even begin to imagine a parentless life, what that must have been like for a young child.

Marilyn proceeds to unlock one door after another. Dark, scary spaces she crawled through, feeling abandoned and alone.

When she's done talking, all I can do is get up and give her a hug. She stiffens.

She hasn't been hugged enough.

There are no words for revelations as significant as what Marilyn just shared with me: the hundred-bed dorm, sewing her own clothes and making her own shoes, the cane marks on her palms if she didn't eat whatever was put on her plate.

My mind recoils. I understand her empty eyes now.

The next day, Marilyn signs up for her four free sessions on the computer. She touches the keys tentatively, like a monster is hiding under each one. Every so often, her finger comes down heavy on the letters and she ends up typing words like 'weeeek' and 'helllloo' and gets all flustered.

'Oh my God! What did I do wrong?' she agonizes while I attempt to calm her down by explaining the use of the 'Backspace' key.

'See, that's how easy it is to undo a mistake on the computer,' I encourage. 'Don't you just love the computer?'

'No, I *don't*,' she is vehement.

In Marilyn's real life, there was no room for 'Backspace' keys. Fenced in by the boundaries of a strict orphanage she had to learn how to do it right – the only way to escape punishment. A quality that defines everything she's ever done, and now does – including punching keys on a computer. From her reactions I understand how terrifying the possibility of an error is to her.

As we spend time together, I learn more. Her sharp, jagged edges are a protective mechanism, the armour she grew to survive a parentless childhood. She has little idea about how to give or receive love. Like the rest of us, however, she needs it as much as the very air she breathes.

I have become the custodian of her life story. In that space, she feels safe to be her own person. She can relax the defences she must erect in her other interactions. If taking computer lessons means spending time with me, she'll do it. To her, it's a legitimate way to receive what she cannot, must not, ask for: attention and affection.

As time goes by, I help create an e-mail account for her. Soon we start to send e-cards to her son who lives in the UK, compose e-mails to her daughter-in-law, and read all the inspirational forwards an erstwhile neighbour sends her. No matter how many times I revisit the tutorial, Marilyn can never remember which keys to push.

'Why isn't the e-mail going?' she asks, irritation crowding into thick lines on her forehead.

'Because you didn't click on "Send", I remind her.

'Where's "Send"?'

'Right there, on top. See?'

She squints and misses, squints and misses, then finally lands her gaze on it.

'It's too confusing,' she grumbles. It's a familiar routine.

'That's why I'm here to help you.'

Slowly, I have her navigate the mouse so the cursor lands on 'Send'. She clicks way too hard, the mouse slides out of position and she ends up clicking on a link that opens a new page.

'Did it go?' she peers at the screen.

'No. Let's try that one more time.'

'Why? What did I do wrong *now*?'

And so we start all over again.

⟨ ⟩

As our friendship blossoms, Marilyn invites me into her apartment. It is a cozy space with plenty of personal touches: cards, photo frames, hand-made dolls and origami.

I discover new, refreshing aspects to her. Beneath the gruff, tough exterior is a sensitive soul that captures life's magical moments on canvas. Her art represents an idyllic world, her only passport to such a universe.

I admire her artwork: paintings of children playing on sun-washed streets; a streetcar ride; towels, sheets and napkins happily aflutter on a washing line; a young woman pushing a buggy while her baby blissfully drowses.

Even as I praise her art, Marilyn starts to complain. 'I can't even hold a paint brush any more.'

'What was it like? Painting these scenes?' I ask, always eager to peer into the window of an artist's imagination.

'Oh, you just set up a canvas and go to work,' she swiftly decimates my carefully constructed fantasy of soul-expression.

Beauty and truth and inspiration have travelled through her now-gnarled fingers to produce wonder on canvas, but any other expression of it is silenced. It is a legacy of her orphanage years. It's a miracle she survived those years.

When her four free lab sessions are done, Marilyn hands me a cheque for ten paid sessions. Given her resistance to working a computer and her constant complaining, I can only presume this is a pretext for closeness and companionship.

Much as I try to quell the pessimist in me, I have serious concerns about these extra lessons. I fear twenty, thirty, forty sessions with me aren't going to enhance her skills enough to send an e-mail on her own. If her memory doesn't fail her, it's her fingers, and if it isn't her fingers, it's her agitated attitude.

This isn't about computer lessons.

Getting clear about this helps me take it nice and easy and slow. Computer literacy isn't the end here. It is sharing space and time with someone who validates her and 'sees' her for who she is. That's what Marilyn needs most, for she has, unfortunately, remained in the shadows for most of her life.

34

WHEN YOU'VE WALKED THROUGH GRIEF, YOU COME OUT A changed person on the other side. For a while, you don't know who you are any more.

I know I have left the other Uma behind, the one who belonged in the world where Amma lived. This new version of me is still unfamiliar, feels awkward, like an ill-fitting garment that hasn't yet moulded to my body or my idea of who I am. This is what my new life looks like, I think, a life where Amma is going to be missing for the rest of my days here.

Grief is its own orchestra. There are swells and dips, ebbs and flows. And the rare moment of truth shines, like the inspired note that even the musician didn't see coming.

On a good day, the veil lifts. My mind is clear. The song of a bird ripples through me, a moment of pure sweetness. Sunshine slants through a green canopy, scattering into gold coins all over the earth, and my heart catches in my throat. It is a split second of magnificence.

My grief is like a window. When it's shut, I'm locked in. When I push it open, feelings and images flow in, and I pulse to the rhythm of life.

My introduction to gratitude as a life-changing concept is through Oprah Winfrey. On many of her shows she has talked about the power of a gratitude journal, a record of life's daily blessings. I make a start in that direction. In my gratitude journal, I faithfully document five blessings before I go to bed, a reminder of all that's going right in my life.

As time goes by, I begin to get used to the idea that Amma is really, truly, finally gone. She's never coming back. I also appreciate the truth that there is meaning in suffering; it is not in vain. When I use my suffering in service, pain can transform into peace and purpose. Being fully present to that truth helps me realize that the rest is a myth – money and power and status as markers of success and security. It is a misguided notion that they can keep a terrible destiny at bay. Nothing is secure; my world is forever changed. In opening up to change and new possibility, I move forward.

In meditation, I begin to wake up to what's real and true. These days I sit for at least twenty minutes without twitching and fidgeting. The more I meditate, the closer I zone in on a critical truth: meditation doesn't have to be yet another marker. The nature of the mind is to drift, to indulge in ceaseless commentary. All I have to do is arrive back here gently, in the here and now: No judgment, no self-berating, no analysis. There is no right or wrong way here. No two experiences of meditation are alike. It is what it is, on the given day. There is nowhere to go, nothing to achieve. Just sit still, breathe in, breathe out and connect with the source of life.

I empty so I can be filled up.

Meditation is its own reward, because it isn't about getting anywhere. It's all about arriving here.

As my connection to God strengthens, I allow stillness to find its way back into my heart. Every time I wrap my arms around an elder, listen to a long-ago story, comfort and lead them out of the thick tangle of sorrow, I am doing what I was unable to for Amma towards the end of her life. There is solace in service, a deep connection as I look beyond the human and begin to see the Divine in every person. For now, that is my true North, in slowly finding my way home to what really matters.

35

AUTUMN LEAVES DRIFT IN COLOURFUL ARCS THROUGH THE morning sunshine. The trees are dressed up for one colourful finalé before they strip down and sink into deep slumber. A rich carpet of greens, golds and reds covers the earth.

The seasons are changing. In tandem, I'm waking up to something inside me shifting, moving, clearing space for a new beginning. The old is being cast off.

I step into the foyer of The Palms thinking these thoughts and sign in. As I put the pen down and turn to see Carol pushing her walker towards me. 'What's it like outside?'

To the seniors in the building I'm their companion, friend, surrogate daughter and weatherman all rolled into one.

'Gorgeous. The colours are just breathtaking,' I say.

'But I mean, is it chilly?' Colours-or-no-colours versus coat-or-no-coat is the primary preoccupation.

'Well, there's a nip in the air,' I offer.

'I don't like it when it gets chilly.'

Carol's summers are too hot, autumns too nippy, winters bitterly cold, and rarely does a spring bring perfect balmy weather. 'Have a nice day,' I say, heading to the elevator.

Today I have an appointment at half-past eleven with Bill who lives on the Assisted Living floor.

Bill can't remember if he brushed his teeth or ate breakfast, but he is a crossword whiz. All I have to say is 'an eight-letter word for event' and in the blink of an eye Bill proudly declares 'Occasion'.

Appa lost his word-identification function and used to keep asking for 'bread' when he wanted his toothbrush, and we would gnash our teeth in frustration.

I'm amazed by the mysterious circuitry of the human brain, which lets short-term memory neural pathways run amuck while preserving word files perfectly.

An avid reader, Bill is well-supplied by his daughter who works at a library. In his living space, there's a book on every surface – coffee table, bedside table, dining table.

Bill's affinity for the computer is tied in to a single reason: the online crossword puzzle website I introduced him to. It's the one tiny grid of his life where he has control. Never mind that he never remembers a puzzle grid we filled up the last time; he tackles it with the fresh enthusiasm and challenge of a toddler who's building a tall tower with bricks.

It's like Appa who reads three-day-old newspapers and insists it's today's news.

Like most people his age, Bill has trouble navigating the mouse. Getting it to go where he wants it, and do what he wants it to, is a struggle, a task he's happy to leave to me these days.

It wasn't always this way. His heated protests that I coddle him led me to surrender the mouse.

Soon, it dawned on him that the game would be far more enjoyable and much less stressful if he relaxed his grip on the mouse. It happened one afternoon as he pushed the mouse around and clicked on a word clue. By some strange quirk of cyber wizardry he landed on the home page of a casino. A firm believer in the sweat-and-grit route to financial freedom, Bill was deeply offended. It was the perfect moment to gently drop the suggestion that I drive the mouse while he focused on unravelling the puzzle. From then on, we've been best buddies on a winning team.

Bill never remembers our appointment, so I go by his apartment and walk him to the lab. Once he's settled, we start to play.

'Oahu greeting,' I read aloud the first clue.

'Oahu greeting ...' he repeats in a low, soft voice, immediately coming up with 'Aloha'. I click the mouse inside each tile and have him push the right letters on the keyboard.

My eyes scan the grid and zero in on the next clue: 'Society girls'.

What on earth is a four-letter word for Society girls?

'Do you know this one?' I ask Bill.

'Know what? You haven't read me the clue,' he reminds me.

'Oops! Sorry! We're looking for a four-letter word for society girls. What could it be?'

Bill taps his chin with a finger for about two seconds. 'Debs,' he offers.

'Brilliant, Bill.' I am amazed that this eighty-six-year-old, who needs an aide to bathe him and dress him and stand guard to make sure he swallows the right dose of the right pills, still has the ability to sprint to the finish line when it comes to word choices. I have new respect for brain plasticity.

As we're figuring out the next word, Howard's rich baritone reaches me from the far end of the corridor. We're barely done with 14 Down and 38 Across when Howard, the seventh-floor Romeo, is pushing his wheelchair in my direction.

'Look who's here!' he shouts, beaming a brilliant smile at me.

'Hey, Howard! Want to work on a crossword?' I ask.

'Isn't that something a person says when he's angry?'

Dementia has made a new man of Howard, his son tells me. 'He used to be a mean bastard,' he once said, shaking his head in disbelief, his eyes fixed on this new version of dad. 'Now he's gone to a real happy place.'

Within moments, Howard does what he does best – disrupts our cozy cerebral crossword challenge. When Howard is around, the spotlight had better shine on him and him alone. If he spots me working with another member of the male species, he will do all he can to pry me away from what he views as competition.

'Give me ten minutes. We're almost done here,' I plead.

'I don't have ten minutes,' says Howard whose long, languorous days comprise nothing more strenuous than meals and naps.

'Please, Howard.'

'Who's this guy?' he hollers in his most impressive jealous boyfriend tone.

'This is Bill. He lives across from you.'

'Never seen him in my life,' Howard mutters, shooting a dark, dangerous look Bill's way.

Cindy, one of the aides, passes by just that moment so I enlist her help in engaging Howard until Bill's crossword grid is complete.

Twenty minutes later, I send Bill off with a goodbye.

Howard rolls into the lab pushing his wheelchair with both arms. 'You are my sunshine ...' he sings to me. His rich baritone is just the beginning of an impressive wooing toolkit; his daily declarations of undying love professed to me with limpid emotion-drenched eyes, unbelievably sweet.

'So when are we going to Vegas?' he asks. This is a daily question, one that comes my way every single time he spies me. 'Come, let's run away from this boring place. Think about it, just you and me in Vegas havin' a ball.'

'I can't go to Vegas. I can't afford it.'

'Oh, don't worry about money, honey. I'll take care of everything. Leave it to me.'

'Well, what about my husband and daughter?'

'You're married!?' an injured pride creeps into his eyes.

This is a familiar routine in the world of dementia. Every single day that I remind him, I jilt him all over again. His pain and abandonment are utterly real. This is beginning to feel like daily punishment I'm meting out.

And then, Howard's surge of bravado takes over. 'Leave the guy. I'll show you a good time. You'll never wanna go back to him,

I promise you that.' He winks at me as I wonder how to escape his love net.

'Do you want to work on the computer?' I ask, trying to find an avenue for distraction. 'Let's type up that song you were singing to me.'

'Nah!' he swats the suggestion away. 'I wanna look into your beautiful eyes and kiss ...'

'Alright, alright. That's enough.' I put my hands up, staunching the flow of his verbal outpouring.

'Come on, Howie, time for lunch.' One of the aides bustles in and starts to manoeuver his wheelchair away from me.

Thank God for the few perfect timings in life.

'What's for lunch today?' Howard asks, anticipation enlivening his voice.

I let out a whoosh of air and sink into my chair. When I accepted this position I had a completely different idea of the challenges I'd face in an ordinary computer lab.

36

For every senior who invites me into her apartment eager for a listening ear, there is another who hobbles away when she sees me approaching. To them, I am the 'computer lady', the toddler's equivalent of the parent who shoves veggies down your throat. Even though I've never believed in steamrolling seniors with a sales pitch, to them I belong in the same category as telemarketers and troublesome traders.

As I walk around the building, camera in hand, clicking pictures of residents to update the 'Resident Photo Directory', I spot a gentleman sitting at a corner table in the dining hall, frowning into his coffee.

I enter the dining hall, approach him and say, 'May I take your picture so we can include you in the Resident Directory?'

Nothing prepares me for the fury with which he turns on me. Venom dripping from his voice, he barks, F... off from here, or I'll ...' and grabs a fork.

I'm not eager to hear the rest of that sentence. I flee.

Another afternoon, I find a lady sitting alone by the library. I introduce myself and moments later she is telling me the apple-picking adventures of her idyllic childhood.

The next time I run into her, I say hello. This time, she shouts, 'I have nothing to tell you, do you hear me?' I can only surmise that an afternoon spent delving into the pleasant memories of her past has also dredged up some unpleasant ones. She sees me as the person who stirred that pot.

A couple of months later, I learn that her husband has passed away. I knock on her apartment door to see how she's coping. The door opens. When she sees me, her features harden.

'What is it?' she demands, anger thickly laced in her voice.

'I just came by to ... to see how you're doing, and ...'

'I told you to leave me alone,' she yells. The door slams on my face.

I do the only thing I can think of. I write a note and slip it under her door.

'I'm sorry you're going through such a hard time,' I write. 'I just want you to know that I'd be happy to listen if you need someone to talk to.' I include my phone number.

It isn't about me. It never is. This is her emotional baggage, her personal battle. So I do the only thing I can: I show up, and offer myself.

She never calls. I respect her need to be left alone. A few months later, I spot her photo in the library, placed alongside those of others we've lost that month. I say a prayer for her.

That call will never come now. But my peace comes from knowing her torment is over.

37

$\mathscr{I}$ CALL MAYA EVERY SUNDAY. CONNECTING WITH HER ON A weekly basis is not only comforting given our closeness; it's my way of keeping in touch with Appa's life. My conversations with Appa are one-sided and awkward. I have to shout into the phone so he can hear me; his responses are mostly confused. Dementia is stealing this man away, a piece at a time, the father I've known and loved.

After I talk with Appa, Maya gets back on the line. I ask, 'How's he really doing? Does he still miss Amma a lot or is it getting better?'

'Now that she's gone, there's even less reason to get out of bed. Thankfully, he cooperates with Kani,' she says.

After a couple of nurse fiascos, Maya's found a sprightly eighteen-year-old who Appa approves of. Kani monitors his medicine intake, runs errands, cleans the house and does chores. Vijaya Mami, the cook who was hired when Amma was diagnosed, is still on the rolls. She takes charge of the kitchen and makes sure Appa eats a decent meal before she leaves.

'Are you travelling a lot?' I ask Maya.

'I have to. No choice. It makes me feel terrible, though. Leaving him and going off like that.'

'It's your job. You're doing the best you can,' even as I say the words, guilt shafts me. I could've been there to help her. What was the logic in moving a whole continent away!?

My brother-in-law is a wonderful, caring man, but Maya has always been a mother hen, clucking around both our parents.

'Does he ... ask about Amma?'

'For days together he won't. And then out of the blue he'll say: "Is she still travelling? When is she coming back?"'

My throat constricts. I don't know what's more painful: dealing with Amma's passing, or hearing how Appa's declining mental faculties shroud reality with confusion.

'And one day,' Maya continues, 'he looked at Amma's photo in the puja, placed a garland of jasmine on it and talked to her like she was right there. That afternoon, he had a seizure. So we decided to hide the photo. Put it someplace where he can't see it. I don't know what goes on inside his head. But I want him to be safe.'

Over this transatlantic connection, it comes to me how my father is struggling with the loss of his beloved wife of forty-seven years. Unlike us, he's unable to articulate his grief in a coherent fashion. Perplexity surrounding her absence is what probably causes his neural pathways to run amuck. It is a sad, sad truth of life. I wonder how much longer he must suffer the punishment of loneliness.

38

$\mathcal{D}$ECEMBER. SNOW AND WINTER WONDERLAND. FROSTED TREE branches, and the glint of diamond dust on morning sunshine. Fairy lights and Christmas tinsel. Carols and candy canes.

A whole new world unfurls for me. I soak in the delicious smells, tastes and textures of the season of giving.

I have been at The Palms for a full year. A year of sharing and caring, but also one of stretching and growing, a year of pushing through doubts and fears. It sinks in now. I didn't choose this work; I was chosen. The work that I was chosen to do has a sacred quality to it. In doing it, I am being reinvented.

With the changing season, corporate priorities are changing too. The economy, that giant monster, has been creeping up on the financial bottom line. Drastic cuts in hours and wages are announced. Almost overnight, my hours in the building dwindle from a healthy twenty to six a week.

This is a community I adore; this is work I love. And now I'm being told to cut out the frills. No more cozy conversations, fond reminiscences and photo albums. Affection within the framework of the computer lab is all the seniors are going to get.

Mid-December, a new resident named Ginny moves in. Ginny is a small woman with a ton of spunk. She has wiry white hair, the bluest eyes I've ever seen, and lights up like the Magnificent Mile every time she smiles.

I'm doing the rounds introducing the computer programme to new residents when I run into her for the first time. We click, just like a snap of the fingers. She opens her door and lets me right in. Over cookies and tea, she shares an abbreviated version of her life story. It is a healthy sign that her mental faculties are in good order.

Ginny owns a laptop, albeit a temperamental one she's unable to tame. In the following weeks we bond as I struggle to retrieve her lost/forgotten/changed usernames and passwords, Ginny apologizing all the while for the confusion she's created in cyber land.

'You're so lucky to have Pam,' I say, one afternoon, as I'm setting up her Gmail account. 'She's such a good daughter to you.'

The words I speak in complete innocence trigger tears. This proud and funny old woman crumbles right in front of my eyes.

'She really is. But ...' Ginny's wrinkled face shrinks as she starts to sob quietly.

I take her hand in mine. 'Oh, Ginny. Did I say something wrong? I'm sorry.'

'No. It's just that she's so depressed these days. Her marriage is over. She loved him so much, but the b.....d ...' Ginny spits the word out like it's a slimy bug sitting on her tongue. 'Pam found out he's been sleeping with her best friend. She's just devastated.'

I hold out my arms and Ginny leans into them.

'I'm so sorry. I had no idea,' I say, stroking her back.

The sordid details of the affair spill from Ginny's lips. I listen, alternately fascinated and horrified at the edifice of lies that hold a marriage together until something gives and the whole structure comes crashing down.

'You can't tell anyone,' Ginny says.

I nod, suddenly feeling the burden of a heavy secret on my soul.

When I check the time, ninety minutes have gone by. The laptop sits there, a geometric design swirling lazily on the screen. I haven't done a shred of work I'm being paid for. In my books, however, the ninety-minute investment in Ginny's mental relief has been well worth the time.

Each week I show up for our appointment and settle down at

Ginny's laptop with the noblest of intentions. . Soon, Ginny starts to give me an update on Pam's life. She tells me she's being brave for her daughter's sake, but I can see what a toll it is taking on this poor woman.

Ginny is at an age where she needs to relax, feet propped up on an ottoman, a favoured beverage by her side. The break-up of a beloved daughter's marriage is a terrible burden on someone who was likely looking forward to a life that involved nothing more demanding than bingo, coffee with the ladies, and a good book. Instead, now her days and nights are spent agonizing over the next chapter of the drama unfolding in her daughter's life.

'I'm eighty-eight and I don't have the strength for this. But I'm all Pam has.'

My weekly visits are her only solace, she tells me. I encourage her to confide in the community's manager who is responsible for resident welfare. When Ginny looks at me, broken and confused, saying, 'But why? I have you,' I have no intelligent answer.

When I e-mail my time card that week, my supervisor is clearly not pleased. I have billed at least four hours over the permitted six. She lets me off with a light rap on the knuckles, reminding me of the rules. My wages are paid in full. When I submit the same hours the next couple of weeks, it doesn't go down well. Our telephone conversation goes something like this:

'I'm sorry ... but there are all these people who just need to talk,' I say. 'And I end up spending more time with them.'

'Well, I'm looking at your time card and I see that you're consistently billing extra hours for a Ginny Thomas. How'd that happen?' my supervisor asks.

'Ginny's going through a really rough time. Her daughter who's her only relative here is in the middle of a messy divorce, she's depressed, and Ginny has been talking to me.'

'But you're doing sessions with her on the computer, right?'

'That's the intention. We spend about half an hour working and then she starts to talk and cry and ...'

'Uma, you have to learn to keep it professional. You're not her therapist.'

'I know. But what am I supposed to do? Just tell her: I'm here only for your computer lesson, please take your tales of woe somewhere else?' I'm unable to keep the sharpness out of my voice.

'No, that's not what I meant. Get her to talk to Kathy. She's in charge of resident welfare and knows the ...'

'I already tried that. Ginny doesn't want to talk to Kathy. She made me promise I'd tell no one.'

'This is getting way too complicated. You don't have the professional qualifications to deal with this situation. I mean, you're not a counselor.'

Yeah right. I know people who've been screwed up by their shrinks.

I take a deep breath. 'I hear what you're saying, but I can't turn my back on a sobbing resident, can I?'

'Talk to Kathy.'

'That would be a breach of trust. I promised Ginny ...'

'Uma, listen to me. I know your heart. I know your intentions. But you have to draw some firm boundaries here. We can't have you billing extra hours every week.'

So that's what it comes down to: extra hours, extra money.

'Okay, I understand.'

I don't. I never will understand.

None of this makes any sense to me. So that's what it's all about. Six miserable hours on the job. I am seething. I am outraged. What if I don't have the right initials at the end of my name? Does a good heart count for nothing these days? Sometimes, a sacred intention and mindfulness matter more than a bunch of degrees.

What am I going to do with Ginny? Tell her she can't confide in me any more for corporate reasons? Walk away? Abandon her when she's already lost and in need of a friend?

My mind casts back to the days when Andy and I legitimately spent twenty hours or so in the community each week. Was it only a year ago? Andy has moved to a new role. Today, my integrity is on the line. If I toe the corporate line, I'm out of integrity with Ginny. And if I cop out on the company rules, I'm out of integrity anyway. Meat in a sandwich.

Surely, a professionally run senior living community has trained staff to deal with delicate matters, and artfully constructed questionnaires to gently draw out hidden secrets. If they don't know Ginny's story, is it really my fault?

Thoughts whirl around my head as I desperately scrabble for a possible solution. My next appointment with Ginny is a week from now. I have to come up with some kind of a plan, although I haven't the foggiest idea what, right this minute.

⟨⟩⟨⟩⟨⟩

When it presents itself, the idea is plain and simple.

Predictably, Ginny and I spend the first half of our session composing and sending an e-mail to her friend. Then she launches into a fresh update on Pamela's situation. I listen without interrupting her flow. When I leave her apartment nearly ninety minutes later, I know I will bill only the thirty minutes we spent on the computer. This pattern continues for a couple of weeks. No one is hurt. Everyone is served. My time card is pristine. But I know I cannot keep this up forever.

As part of my new job description, I take pictures of new residents and update the photo directory, deliver free tutorial sessions, and plod through mind-numbing paperwork to update community stats. These days, I'm dragging myself to work. There's little energy or enthusiasm for what has dwindled to a purely administrative role.

As months go by and March rolls around, I know in my heart that a decision looms ahead of me. I struggle with it, put it off, hide from it, pretend it isn't real, but it stalks me all the while. The question I must now face is: am I willing to settle for so little?

I didn't sign up for this; it doesn't feel authentic to me.

While my role started out by getting seniors connected in a computer lab, those connections took on a dimension even I hadn't imagined. My experience has taught me that the remedy for loneliness – the reality of the majority of seniors in the community – isn't going to be chased away by connections in cyberspace.

The seniors who know their computer basics or are adventurous enough to learn a new skill are easy to convince. They're open to sitting in front of a computer, and engage meaningfully. The vast majority is not interested in mastering one more challenge to what is an already challenging phase in their lives. That said, they do have a real yearning to connect in other ways. That was a gap I bridged with conversations and story-sharing times. And if the company cannot support that, I'm just going to have to find a way to do it on my own terms.

I know now that not honouring it would amount to straying away from a personal truth.

All this mental meandering leads to one big fear. If I quit my job, will I have access to this building which is almost second home to me now? Can I continue to have a relationship with the seniors I adore? Surely, a new lab assistant will be hired. Will I be viewed as an intruder?

My mind fights the thought of severing my connection with this community. The next couple of days go by in a fog of indecision. I talk myself through all the pros and cons. I journal. I meditate. I pray. And then, I come to a decision.

It's a bright April morning when I request my supervisor for some alone time. She suggests lunch. Over a deliciously warm panini I announce my painful decision.

'I feel like I've come to the end of the road with this position. Six hours just don't cut it for me. More than that, I miss the freedom of interacting with the seniors in a manner that served them. So ... this is it, I guess.' I shrug, look at her and wait for a response.

'I can't even imagine the building without you there,' she says. 'But it is what it is. Times are tough and I know these hours are ridiculous. What can I say?'

'My last day will be 15th of April. I have two weeks to tell the residents and wrap things up.'

Even as I speak the words, the awful thought registers: soon, I'm going to have to break the news to my beloved senior friends.

'That's good. Give us some time to get all the paperwork organized so ...' I realize she's been talking.

'I will miss you,' she says, giving me a hug as we prepare to leave.

She pays for lunch.

39

$\mathcal{I}$T'S DIFFICULT, BUT RARELY IS THERE A PLEASANT WAY TO deliver the truth, no matter the situation. I start by telling the seniors I am closest to that I've handed in my papers. Nothing has prepared me for the outpouring of love and affection that greets this announcement. It rushes at me, a swiftly flowing river.

Tears bloom in my eyes at the love and sentiments that come my way.

'Oh, no. You're my best friend in this building.'

'Who will I talk to?'

'You won't stop coming to see us, will you?'

'Can I keep in touch with you on phone?'

I squeeze their hands in comfort. I hug them. I reassure them that although this feels like abandonment, it definitely is not. They're like family to me, and there's no way I will disappear from their lives.

'What about our Monday group?' one of the members asks me. The decision regarding the fate of our cozy discussion group is in the hands of the community's lifestyle director.

'I'd like to keep it going,' says Dana. 'I mean, if that's still an option for you. The residents love the group and I see no reason why we should let it go.'

I release the breath I've been holding in, a whoosh of pure delight. This was my biggest fear – that my connection to the community would somehow be cut off if I gave up my part-time job. Not only does Dana help me keep the group going, I will be able to visit with my favourite seniors.

'Thank you, Dana,' I throw my arms around her.

I spend the next ten days wrapping up. There is all the paperwork and building stats to update and resident appointments to get through before I leave.

My last Monday in the building. I stand before the seniors to make my final presentation. The words that usually flow easy stick in my throat today. My chest hurts. Heck, this isn't a final goodbye. I live six miles down the road. Besides, I will have a reason to be here every week. Even so, I can't help feeling that this is the end of a chapter as I've known it. I don't know what it is, but something is shifting.

'… I owe so much to each one of you for inviting me into your apartments and your hearts, for sharing your stories with me.'

My eyes land softly on Janice. *I hope someone will continue to play computer games with her.*

'… this has been an incredible learning curve for me. Coming from a different culture, working with you folks …'

I spot Renee in the second row. *She always called me when she couldn't find the website she was looking for.*

'… learning about Ellis Island and the Great Depression and your experiences first-hand … what a gift!'

Margaret looks at me, then looks away. *Does she see this as betrayal?*

It won't be the same, not being the weatherman, mailman, errand girl, companion. It's time to go, to walk away from this chapter, and towards the beginning of the next. There is sadness, anticipation and trepidation, a giant cauldron of emotions bubbling inside me.

Embrace change, my heart whispers.

I close my eyes and take a deep breath, knowing I must trust what's next for me.

40

$\mathcal{I}$T IS JULY 2010. EIGHTEEN MONTHS SINCE MY EMINENTLY forgettable last trip to India. Our tickets – Ruki's and mine – are booked to travel again.

Appa's older, frailer, and lonelier. I feel the significance of the sand slipping through the hourglass.

In the weeks leading up to our travel, we traipse miles of mall aisles, buying gifts for friends and family. When all is done and our bags are packed, excitement begins to course through me once again.

On the airplane, I allow myself to feel joy. *I will be in Chennai soon. It's going to be a good trip this time.*

It is the wee hours of the morning when we disembark at Chennai International Airport. People throng the visitors' area, rose garlands in hand, to greet loved ones; yuppies stroll through the passenger terminal, engrossed in their iPhones and iPads.

Maya and Guru are part of the crowd, albeit without the rose garlands. I spot them and wave, the anticipation of a vacation now real.

Ancient traditions and modern-day chaos define India best. As we weave through knots of people, honking cars, disorderly traffic, high-decibel chatter and the smells of exhaust fuel and rotting food in the air, I know I'm home.

This is India. This is home.

On the drive home, Ruki and Maya are talking up a storm when the thought comes to me.

This is India. This is home. This is not home.

This will never be home in the way it used to be. The home

where Amma and Appa lived together as one unit, the harbour all my sibling ships docked at, the home base of my entire life until this moment. Just like that, with that single thought, everything is changed.

I try to let Maya's excited chatter distract me from this depressing conclusion. When there's a lull in the conversation, my mind wanders back to the 'what-if land'. How different this scenario might have been if Amma had been home, waiting to receive us.

Sleep-bleary eyes, animated chatter, early morning light leaking into the house, a hundred questions about America spilling from her eager lips. Fresh milk and dark decoction melding into the magical taste of home-made coffee. Stories of relatives and friends and neighbours. Laughter and jokes and hugs. What-shall-I-make-for-lunch debates and suggestions.

A sudden emptiness surrounds me. That is now a memory, just a memory.

I'll never have that, ever again.

It is four in the morning when we arrive home. Appa is asleep, so we tiptoe and whisper as we set our bags down.

This is my first time in Maya and Guru's new, compact apartment – two bedrooms, a living area and a tiny kitchen. Appa has one bedroom; Maya and Guru have the other. Kani sleeps on a mattress she spreads on the floor in Appa's bedroom. Ruki and I will use the living space as sleeping quarters.

As Maya turns on the kitchen light to make coffee, Appa hobbles out to the living room. He gives me a big hug, says, 'I've been waiting for you.'

In that moment, everything feels right. My father needs me. And I still need him.

By evening, I'm missing what I've come to think of as 'Amma's house' so much that I suggest we take a walk to the neighbourhood where the building stands. Ruki, Maya and I set off navigating swerving cyclists, pedestrians, speeding cars, reckless autorickshaws and the assortment of roadside vendors and peddlers, an integral feature of India's street life. As we walk past flower-sellers threading sweet-smelling jasmine and bright yellow marigolds into pretty garlands, sadness washes over me. The smells and sights and sounds that used to be an essential part of my life in a Chennai suburb remind me how everything has changed. Amma's absence is all-pervasive. It's like the very air we're breathing is now different.

Before I know it, I'm there, right outside the black gates. I stand and stare, an orphan. Beyond the wall, I see the familiar black metallic grille. This is the exact spot where I used to park my scooter. From here, I could see Amma sitting on the divan and sipping coffee, through the open front door, her eyes riveted on some domestic drama playing on television.

I blink my eyes. The drapes are drawn. The grille door that was always open – allowing fresh sea breeze to waft through the apartment – is shut.

'Aunty next-door says,' Maya's voice cuts in, 'the folks that live here now always keep the door shut. Remember how Amma …'

My bobbing head emphasizes that indeed I do remember every single detail.

What I once thought of and referred to as 'Amma's house' is now someone else's home. Nothing of what I know or remember lives there any more. Everything about that space – the bright orange window drapes, the divan with its soft, sagging mattress, the circular chocolate-brown dining table, pots and pans in the kitchen, Appa's dhoti fluttering on the makeshift clothesline, Amma's creams and lotions lined up on the dresser – exists only in memory.

'Let's go,' I say, never wanting to come back here ever again. It's a place I no longer recognize. It has no relevance to my life any more. Somewhere inside of me, a door closes.

41

*T*HAT NIGHT, JET LAG KEEPS ME WIDE AWAKE. I'M TOSSING around restlessly on a hot mattress on the living room floor, envious of Ruki who's fast asleep on the divan.

Toss, turn, shift. Re-position pillow. Toss. Re-position pillow again – 1 a.m., 2.30 a.m., 2.45 a.m. – I'm still wide awake.

Moments later, I hear a shuffling noise. Instantly alert, I peer into the darkness. A shadowy figure comes towards me. It's Appa.

He enters the living room, calls out for Maya. I sit up in bed. He's forgotten I'm here already.

'It's me, Uma.'

'Uma?'

'What is it, Appa?'

'When did you come?'

That piece of information has vanished as reliably as what he ate for dinner last night. Slowly, he inches towards the cane sofa. I quickly shove the corners of my mattress out of his way. It's cramped enough with me wedging a mattress between the divan and the furniture in the living room.

Pale moonlight leaks a milky light through the drapes. The windows are wide open, but the night air is still.

Appa settles down on the sofa, a worried frown on his face. 'What happened to our property in Hyderabad?' he asks. 'Where are the papers? I can't find them.'

Now I'm the one with amnesia. I have a vague memory of an investment my father made when I was in my twenties. As far as I recall, Amma handled the sale of that land in Hyderabad with my uncle's assistance.

'You remember Sriram and Amma completed the sale?' I jog his memory.

'No, no. We never sold that land,' he says. 'The property is in my name. I didn't sign any papers.'

I'm wide awake at three, but a disagreement about a piece of land we owned many moons ago is not what I want to engage in.

'Appa, it's three in the morning. May be you should go to sleep. We can discuss this tomorrow morning.'

'Oh, I'm usually up early. I'll make some coffee.'

He prepares to get up.

I jump to my feet, dissuade him, and confidently pronounce he can do that a couple of hours later, fully convinced that it will be forgotten. He resists for a while, but I stand my ground. Eventually, he gives in and lets me escort him into the bedroom. I help him into bed, and pull the sheet up, casting a disapproving look Kani's way. As if to mock me she lets out a soft snore, blissfully unaware of Appa's dawn meanderings.

I return to my makeshift bed and wait for sleep to come get me.

Over the next five days, Appa is up at an unearthly hour every night. I am too. Jet lag has a tight grip on me. I sleep the sleep of the dead in the afternoons and struggle with insomnia at night.

One night, I hear cricket commentary drifting from Appa's room, the blue hazy shadows of the television screen shifting on the mosaic floor. The commentator's Australian accent is like an ECG graph. It zigzags in tempo with the action on the field.

A few minutes later, I hear the soft tap-tap-tapping of Appa's cane growing louder as he approaches the living room.

I sit up in bed.

'Appa ...'

'I'm going to make some coffee.'

'It's two in the morning. Too early for coffee.'

This time, he listens. Slowly, he sits down on the cane sofa beside my mattress.

'I don't know where she is,' he says. 'I can't find her.'

My stomach squeezes. I know he's talking about Amma. I don't quite know how to respond. As my mind scrabbles for the right words, he starts talking again.

'She went on a trip. But she didn't tell me when she's coming back.' He shakes his head. 'May be she did. I must've forgotten.'

Maybe I should've let him make that coffee.

I'm trying to think of a topic of distraction, but my sleep-addled brain is swaddled in thick cotton-wool at two in the morning.

He looks at me, 'Did she tell you?'

His question flips a switch in my brain. Now I have to come up with something.

'Um ... I ... think it'll take her some time,' a lame, limp, damp squib excuse.

Ruki shifts in her bed, a dark mass of movement.

Appa squints. 'Who's that?' he points his cane at the bed. 'Over there?'

'Ruki.'

'Oh, she came with you,' he smiles. 'Nice, nice.'

'Come, Appa. Let's get you back in bed. It's late.'

He lets me. I hold him by the upper arm, lead him to bed, tuck him in and return to my bed.

Five minutes later, the loud snores puncturing the stillness of night tell me it's mission accomplished for tonight.

When this nocturnal routine continues for five nights in a row, I simply decide to flow with it. I hear Appa's footsteps, his head pokes through the door, I get up and pat the cane sofa, encouraging him to sit down. We end up having a nice little chat. Then I take him back to bed.

Five days later, Ruki and I are on a night train to Mysore, home to her paternal grandparents, aunt and uncle. We're taking a week-long vacation with them.

42

Two days later, we're in an amusement park with Ruki's older cousin and his wife when my cell phone rings. I fish around in my bag, grab my phone. 'Hello?'

It's Maya.

'Appa's in hospital.'

My heart stands still for a second.

'What happened? He was fine when we left.'

'He developed a severe urinary infection,' she says. 'He's been running a fever with chills and the doctor advised that he be admitted without delay.'

Appa is in intensive care.

My week-long vacation vanishes right before my eyes. *Should I head back home? But that's so unfair to my in-laws who're seeing us after two whole years and have been looking forward to this time with us.*

Maya reassures me. There's no need to rush to Chennai, she'll keep me posted. The familiar feeling of inadequacy creeps upon me. What is it with my parents? I turn my back and they launch straight into crisis mode.

The next five days are all about willing time to hurry. My physical self is in Mysore and the rest of me inside that intensive care unit in Chennai. I'm surrounded by people and distracted by outings, but I just want this week to be over so I can head home and be with Appa.

I call Girish; Girish calls Maya; Maya calls me. Most of the time I'm on the phone; the status reports and updates on Appa are not too encouraging. When Ruki and I board the train back to Chennai, I can't wait for the night to be over. After some fitful tossing and turning, I'm thankful when light paints the sky. I press my nose to the glass, relieved to spot the mustard-yellow sign – 'Chennai Central' – in black lettering outside my window.

We get home, I shower, and Guru drives me to the hospital.

Maya is with Appa.

This was supposed to be a vacation!

The thought flitting through my head makes me feel like a traitor. But the time I thought I'd be spending with my father certainly did not involve a hospital room, an oxygen machine, doctors and orderlies.

As we pull up outside the hospital, I have a moment.

It's the same hospital they rushed Amma to, where she was pronounced dead on arrival.

As the idea sinks in, my breakfast slowly makes its way up my throat. It's the same space, the same fear, the same despair. Disinfectant-laced air, white-uniformed nurses, paint peeling off the walls, endless grey corridors.

I don't want to be here. I need to be here. Appa needs me. Maya needs me.

It's a familiar story, a known plotline unfolding. Déjà vu.

When I walk into the ICU, Maya is coaxing Appa to eat some oatmeal. As usual, he's fussing. She gives me a welcome-back hug. 'Want to try?' she asks, holding out the bowl. I accept it. Appa keeps his lips tightly pursed, like a stubborn toddler.

'Appa,' I say. 'I came all the way from Mysore just to feed you.' It works like magic. His lips part tentatively, then he opens his mouth wide to receive a spoonful of oatmeal.

'Oh, I see now. She's the favourite daughter. That's the advantage if you live in Chicago,' Maya kids him. Together, we're able to tease a thin smile out of him.

Maya gathers her things, goes home to take a break, shower and grab some lunch. Before she leaves, we exchange a look that says we're-back-in-the-trenches-soul-sisters.

Over the next week, Appa's descent is swift. His kidneys are failing. His physician, Dr S. K., is one of the most generous men of medicine I have ever met. A man of genuine compassion, he considers the health crisis from all angles, utterly different from professional specialists who deliver a cold prognosis unmindful of family dynamics.

Mahesh is back in the loop and calls from Chicago for daily updates. Vidu and I planned our vacations to coincide, so she arrives a week later with my six-year-old nephew, Abu. While Ruki babysits her little cousin and finds amusing ways to entertain him, we three sisters rotate hospital shifts.

Appa is now increasingly restless. He yanks off his oxygen mask, tugs at the IV tubes, and tries to get out of bed. His food intake drops steadily to the point where he's drinking only coffee and buttermilk.

When Mahesh calls next, I tell him it's time to book his ticket.

The ICU is strict about visitor entry rules. Only one family member is allowed by the patient's bedside. But the nurses, seeing that Appa is sinking, flex the rule for us. Most times they allow two of us; occasionally all three sisters hover over Appa, talking, feeding, cajoling and rubbing his feet.

Here we are, bonding over an ailing parent, all over again. Now that he is in the last throes of his earthly battle, together we decide to place Amma's photo on his bedside table. Appa turns his head slowly, stares at Amma's photo. He gazes at her, unblinking. *I'd give anything to know what's going through his mind.*

When we get home we sit in a prayer circle, Amma's photo placed in the middle, and pray for Appa's peaceful release. We ask her to ease his transition and receive him gently on the other side. In the hospital, we stand in a circle and hold hands around Appa's bed, giving him permission to leave, promising him that we will look out for each other.

Since the road accident and brain injury, it has been a seventeen-year struggle for Appa. It is painful to have to stand by and watch him gasp for every breath now.

Waiting is hard. When we can control outcomes we feel capable and there is a path to follow. But no one can speed the end of a life. And so we wait, as patiently as we can, one moment at a time.

The three of us – Maya, Vidu and I – only go home to shower, eat and sleep. Our conversations are all about injections, pharmacy bills and doctor's fees. I think I'd feel better if Ruki protested about it, at least a little. That she accepts everything with remarkable stoicism only sharpens my guilt.

I can't believe I'm doing this to her all over again – even when we're visiting from the other side of the world.

43

$\mathcal{M}$AHESH FLIES INTO CHENNAI IN THE EARLY HOURS OF
1 August, and drives straight to the hospital. When he walks into
the ICU, steps up to Appa's bed and leans over him, Appa's lips
stretch in a wan smile of recognition.

As news of Appa's discouraging prognosis travels through the
family grapevine, batches of relatives descend on the hospital to
say goodbye. It's becoming a tiresome exercise, stalling the flow.

Mahesh takes over the night vigil. Although it's not strictly
necessary, he opts to spend the nights sleeping on a wooden bench
outside the ICU. One of us gives him a break in the morning.

On 6 August, Dr S. K. decides to move Appa to a small private
room.

Girish flies into Chennai the next morning, a Saturday. That
afternoon, Vidu, Maya and I are gathered at Appa's bedside. We
spend a memorable few hours singing the songs of our childhood,
the songs Appa taught us. We take turns at rubbing his feet. We
hold his hand and talk to him. By now, he's not too responsive,
but every time one of us calls 'Appa ...' there's a flicker in his eyes.

The domestic set up is straining at the seams with nine people
living out of three rooms. So, Girish suggests that we spend
Saturday night at the company guest-house.

At nine in the morning on Sunday, the phone rings.

'Ums,' Maya calls me by my nickname. 'He's gone,' she
whispers.

'Oh, poor Appa,' I sigh. 'What can I say? I'm sad. But I have to
say I'm also relieved his suffering is over.'

I tell her we'll get to the hospital in half an hour. I hang up, and the tears come.

This is what it feels like to be orphaned.

I take a moment, let the thought sink in. Girish and I finish packing, pick up our bags and step outside the guest-house to hail an autorickshaw.

Although it's a Sunday, the roads are choked with traffic. We bump along in a rickety rickshaw, shouting to be heard above the din of a typical India ride: honking cars, noisy motorcycles, and loudspeakers blaring Tamil film music.

The autorickshaw parks at the kerb outside the hospital. Climbing over the metal railings of the rickshaw, I sprint towards the hospital steps. A voice reminds me: *There's no need to rush. The life has gone out of Appa's body.*

Ignoring the voice, I rush up the stairs and run into Appa's room.

Appa looks like he's fast asleep, more peaceful in death than in life. He looks young, if that's possible, the lines on his forehead smoothed out. It is such a contrast to the labours of his last ten days, the sheer effort to drag breath into his lungs which caused his face to tighten, twitch and tense.

Unlike when Amma passed away, all four of us kids are here this time. The gifts we were able to give Appa – our presence, love and care – fill me with a sense of peace. At last, Amma and Appa are together again, just the way both would want it.

The menfolk dress Appa's body in traditional garb, in readiness for cremation. Relatives stream in and out of the hospital room. Appa's only surviving sibling, his older sister, walks into the room like the floor is made of eggshells. Her face is a picture of sorrow.

'I was fifteen when he was born. He was more my baby than my younger brother,' she says. I've grown up basking in the warmth of their special affection for each other.

Now she stands by his bed, watches him for a long time, and

dabs the tears at the corners of her eyes. With Appa gone, she's the only sibling left.

Unlike when Amma passed away, this time we siblings take charge of the proceedings. The body is not going home because it's going to be impossible to get him up three flights of stairs. Maya's apartment building has no elevator; it's also way too small for the purification rituals.

Emboldened, I climb into the ambulance, sit beside Appa's body and ride to the crematorium. Something about this time is different. Appa needs all of us till the very end.

Off to the side of the crematorium is a large hall and an expanse of tiled floor where the priest carries out the death rituals, after we bathe the body. Mahesh performs the last rites, a son's duty to ensure a parent's salvation.

Appa's mortal remains slide into the waiting mouth of the incinerator.

Goodbye, Appa.

The sadness is everywhere, a giant cloud of feelings. There's also relief, this time.

While the rest of us head home to take purifying baths, Mahesh must wait for the ashes. A male elder will accompany him to the seashore where he will chant the final mantras before scattering Appa's ashes.

It is four in the evening when we get home. Baths, food, condolence calls from family and friends, melancholy.

As soon as I have a private moment, I find my gratitude journal. I cast my mind back over the past two weeks, and the blessings that abounded in the face of my father's slow and painful death. If I don't record them right now, they'll be lost to me forever. I start to write down the blessings as they come to me.

I'm grateful that the four of us bonded and worked as a team, supporting and comforting each other through this difficult time. I'm grateful Appa experienced this coming together of his four children when he most needed us. I'm grateful for all the financial contributions that came in to ease the situation.

When I finish, I end up with twenty-five.

Another chapter in my life is over. The page is turned.

—◁◦◦◦▷—

Three days after Appa's passing, I suggest to my siblings that we go out for a meal. Eating out within days of one's bereavement is not acceptable within the framework of tradition. But I know in my heart that Amma's and Appa's spirit will rejoice as they watch their four children bond over a meal.

We choose an intimate Italian restaurant for our new beginning. Over dinner, each of us take turns to own up for our part in the breakdowns of the past and apologize. We make a commitment to look out for each other.

It is an evening to remember.

'Why don't you stay in Chennai longer this time?' Girish suggests. 'When Amma passed away, Ruki was in the middle of her sophomore year and you had to rush back, remember?'

'Yeah, but Ruki's school starts on—' I try to offer a counter argument.

'—I'll just put off all travel till you get back. Take time to grieve Appa. Spend time with your sisters,' says my husband who is the most generous human being I know.

I could use this break. I need to grieve my father. I need my sisters.

I change my return date and decide to stay back in Chennai an extra month. Vidu decides to stay two more weeks. We put this time of togetherness to good use. We share favourite Appa stories, laugh and cry together. We empty out his closet, bag all his belongings and send them to a lady who runs a halfway home for AIDS victims.

The day his bed is taken away – the one with the green metal railings – I feel that Appa has really moved out, moved on to another realm. This is the end. That last piece of furniture moving out shuts the door on an era called caring for our parents.

The thirteenth day after his passing is a celebration of the release of his spirit. We sponsor lunch for the inmates of an old age home. The three of us get there early so we can serve the inmates and take their blessings, a gesture of benevolence and care.

Once Vidu and Abu leave Chennai, time hangs heavy. Two more weeks before I fly out to Chicago. Maya and Guru are swallowed up by their jobs. I'm rattling around alone in the apartment, left with my thoughts of how empty life seems with both Amma and Appa gone.

I'm ready to head back home.

44

$\mathcal{I}$T IS SEPTEMBER 2010. I ARRIVE IN CHICAGO TO BALMY FALL weather: crisp autumn leaves, mild sunshine, the smell of wood smoke and a gentle nip in the air.

Amma passed away in the winter; Appa, in the fall. Spring and summer are, thankfully, intact.

Over the next weeks and months, Mahesh and I reconnect and reconstruct a new relationship. Forgiveness is a beautiful thing. Hard as it is to seek and deliver, it brings precious rewards.

The brother I've known and loved all my life emerges, bit by bit. The shared language of our childhood – a history we've created growing up – was never forgotten. We just hadn't practiced it in a while.

I love the man my brother is today. I love his family. We talk and laugh and eat and reminisce together.

In experiencing the power of forgiveness, I know that we can never create a new beginning by holding on to the energy of the past. It is only possible to birth a new story by beginning anew – in this moment.

And anyone who dreams of a new beginning knows they must first wake up.

———<<>•<>•<>>———

After the first flush of my reunion with Girish, it is back to the business of living. Ruki is in her senior year of high school; her parents are caught up in the frenetic world of admission essays, grants, scholarships, college choices and letters of recommendation.

Work continues to be the scaffolding of my husband's life. He is fuelled by a new purpose, driven by an ambitious dream, common to every immigrant: the dream of sending his child to an American university. We're perched on the cusp of that dream.

Ruki is keen to go to a small, private liberal arts college. The desire is well-aligned with her shy personality and academic bent of mind. And an achievable goal, given her A-heavy report card. My heart swells with pride as I think back to her transition from the gawky fourteen-year-old into a confident seventeen-year-old young woman. In less than a year, she will fly the coop. She's still my little girl. She isn't. She even hates being called that.

In complete contrast to the rest of my family's drive and ambition, a hollow emptiness echoes inside me. I suffer from a total lack of motivation, the internal fire needed to go on a job hunt.

I have no desire to rush through a morning commute, go to a job and earn money for its own sake. Is this me, I have to wonder. I, who performed exceedingly well for two decades in a fiercely competitive advertising industry, always valued independence and earned my own money since graduating from college. All the jobs I've had so far have brought in more success, validation and money than I'd ever imagined. Now, the desire to compete on that playing field has vanished like a puff of smoke.

Estranged from the rest of the world and what everyone considers normal rituals of living, I struggle through one of my loneliest phases. Since Amma's passing, I feel like a person who's been taken apart and put back together, with brand new programming. The old software doesn't serve me any more.

Life's big questions push my safe boundaries, challenge my comfort zone. A one-word mantra takes up residence inside my head.

Serve. Serve. Serve.

My life beats to the rhythms of a different drummer.

Make a difference. Make every day of your life count.

I don't understand it; I have no choice but to obey that compelling voice. One thing I do know for sure. It's a hellishly lonely place to be in.

I find my biggest teacher in Dr Wayne Dyer and begin to immerse myself in his books. They speak a language I feel companioned by. It is like going to the University of Life. The wisdom between the pages elevates me to a new way of thinking and being.

In *The Shift: Taking Your Life from Ambition to Meaning*, Dr Dyer talks about a person's transition from the morning of life where the main player is the ego to the afternoon of life where 'meaning' replaces 'ambition'. My heart beats *yes, yes, yes.*

The truths of the Tao speak to me so eloquently, and yet, they are truths the world scoffs at. The Tao's messages – accomplish much by trying less, shift from acquisition and pursuit to self-mastery, eliminate competition from your life and retreat into quiet strength, and do nothing so you can have everything – resonate with me in a profound way. From the Buddhist teacher, Tara Brach, I learn that *dukka* stems from attachment, that non-attachment is the route to peace; Oprah Winfrey has always preached this simple truth from the pulpit of her show: the greatest joy lies in causing others to experience joy.

The messages are unrelenting. They fly in at me from all directions. As I tune into Dr Dyer's weekly radio show one afternoon, I hear ten words that stick in my mind like a fly to flypaper.

Don't let money be the reason why you don't serve.

No matter how hard I try, I cannot unstick those words.

The exhortation drowns everything else out. It smothers all logic, reason and common sense. It refuses to acknowledge the reality of federal loans and college tuition.

Dr Dyer is out to get me today, I know, as I listen to his next words.

The only thing you can do with this life is to give it away.

Even as the words settle into my brain, an image of Amma's body flashes through my mind. *She took nothing with her; she just gave away everything she had.*

Yet, the essence of who she is lives on in us, her children, and every soul she touched during her earthly journey. Eighteen months after her passing, the flower-seller and ironing woman still speak of her in reverential whispers. That is what lives on, long after the physical form is shed.

It is compelling, this inner voice. It pulls and tugs at my heart. It won't let me be.

Serve from the purest place within you.

45

 $\mathcal{T}$ HREE MONTHS HAVE PASSED SINCE I RETURNED FROM INDIA. I am making no move towards finding a job and have been dodging my husband's hints and queries. How do I tell a Type A guy that my heart's calling is to serve, that I cannot follow two masters so I must choose between God and money. How do I find the words to convey that the only thing we leave behind is the essence of who we are and what we mean to those we serve.

I have been tossing words in my head, trying to come up with a plausible explanation for my decision – especially at a time when Ruki is eight months shy of graduating from high school.

I pray. I compose words in my head. I plan on delivering my little speech. I chicken out. I pray some more. I shed tears of frustration. I meditate. I plead with God to show me an escape route. The words have fled. I know I'm empty on the job-hunt front, but I'm full of purpose.

Inevitably, Girish intends to find the answers he's been patiently waiting for.

'I don't understand it,' he begins. 'Most of the world works. There are bills to pay. People volunteer in their free time. I know you've lost Amma and Appa and things haven't been easy for you after moving ... but, Ruki's getting ready to go to college ... there's the mortgage, the car payments ... I mean, I don't need to be telling you all this. You know our situation.'

The voices in my head are having a field day with this.

You're a loser. You don't care about your family. You're selfish and self-centred. You want this poor man to carry the burden all by himself. What kind of a wife and mother are you? And on and on and on.

It's been a struggle, I admit. My three trips to India in two years have been a drain on the family coffers. To add to that, I've been unemployed for eight months. It isn't a story of financial ruin, but looming ahead is a college tuition fee.

I steal a glance at Girish, then quickly look away. Not once in twenty years of married life has my husband told me he's disappointed in me or my decisions, but I hear it in his voice now. What's worse, I understand it, but feel powerless to fix it. The edge of frustration, of being unable to comprehend a truth that's vastly different from everything he's ever known and been raised to believe in. This probably feels like abandonment to him.

In another world, we were true partners, both marching towards common goals, hand in hand: Ruki's education, money for retirement, a little vacation stash. Now, I've disengaged my hand from his, to take a completely unplanned life detour. There's a part of me that understands his confusion. There's a part of me that doesn't quite know how to explain my predicament. There's a part that suffers the guilt of bailing out on him. Although I know in the purest place of my being that following my inner guidance system cannot be a mistake, an accident, a random phase that's happening in my life.

He is waiting for me to speak.

'I … I don't know what to say,' I turn away.

It's the same old, same old. I've been saying this, and I know it's not enough. I'm going to have to do better. So I take a deep breath and plunge into icy waters, swimming upstream.

'Ever since Amma died,' I begin, 'something's changed. Something's shifted for me. I didn't ask for this to happen. It just has. I feel this calling in my heart. And I'm not able to turn away from it. It's as if God or the universe is moving me towards something. I don't know what that is yet, but I feel this powerful need to serve.'

Girish looks at me for a moment, then laughs. In that laugh is a combination of pain, anger, disillusionment and confusion. I can tell it is not a laugh he enjoys.

'So, God doesn't want you to serve your family,' he says, the acid in his voice unmistakable.

'No. I mean, that's not what ...' I stumble over the rocky terrain of word choices.

'We have two mortgages, one here and one in Chennai. Do I really have to explain all this to you?'

My throat hurts. My gut twists. The truth is, I cannot argue with anything my husband has just said. I simply stand, frozen, mute. The words are colliding inside my chest.

I didn't choose this life. I didn't plan on losing both Amma and Appa within twenty-eight months of moving to Chicago. You think I'm enjoying this!? You think I'm doing this to be selfish and cruel and inconsiderate? My world has turned upside down. I don't even know who I am any more. It's like my skin is peeling off and I'm discovering there's another layer to me. I'm seeing what's really true for me. So don't ask me these questions. I don't know how to answer you. Ask God.

I push the words down my angry throat to a place deep within, bury them inside my chest and behind my rib cage. My husband is still waiting, his face full of questions.

'All of us would love to follow our dreams,' he continues, 'and do what we love. But that's not how life works. You get up each morning, put on your work face and go to the job you have so your family has a roof over their head and food in their belly.'

Every word contains a sting of venom.

'What happens to this family if I wake up one day and decide I've had enough and don't want to go to work? Do I even *have* that choice?'

'I didn't choose this; it chose me,' I say quietly. My husband's face is a blank canvas. 'If that makes any sense,' I add.

He merely shrugs, the slump of defeat etched in his shoulders.

Every attempt to explain the path I'm walking ends in similar fashion. The argument simply runs out of steam and dead-ends.

We hit the proverbial wall. We back off. We go our separate ways. Stony silence grows thick between us. Until the next time. The next bill. The next trigger. And we engage in a new variation of the same argument.

'What happens if I lose my job?'

'What happens if I drop dead?'

'What happens if we can't afford Ruki's college tuition?'

My head hurts, my bones ache, my spirit is weary.

But when I step inside the nursing home where I volunteer and my fingers knead away the knots in Nora's neck, or rub lotion into Barb's dry hands or wipe the tears running down Teresa's face, I am alive and present and full of purpose. I'm in a bubble where all that matters is love, the giving and receiving of it. I experience God's grace flow through my being and my heart sings with a joy that is not of this world.

Gut feelings are hard to put into words. Gut feelings have no container. That is my problem. I am unable to fashion these feelings into logical words and sound rationale that will convince my driven, striven husband who lives by the rules of the real world. A good husband, a good father, a good man just doing the best he can to keep us all afloat. What saddens me is that he thinks I'm trying to drown our little catamaran.

46

$\mathcal{I}$ EASE THE CAR INTO THE NURSING HOME'S PARKING LOT. IT'S my volunteering day. As is my practice before I climb out of the car, I join my palms together at the heart and seek guidance. *God, how may I serve you today? Lead me where you need me to go.*

I walk towards the building, anticipation building up. *Who will I get to serve today?* It amazes me how I am always sent to the right person at the right time. Simply asking, and going with the flow, not seeking to control anything or any one – there's a world of wisdom in that simple truth.

A warm whoosh of air envelops me as the automatic doors slide open. I stop at the front desk, sign in the register and give Sandy a little wave. She's engaged in a serious phone conversation.

Smells of urine and staleness float in the air. I walk down the hallway, glancing at name signs posted outside doors, all the while paying attention to the soul nudge that tells me where to go. When I trust my intuition, my feet usually walk into the right room. I've never known how, but it's always perfect. The resident in that room has a need that I'm called to meet.

Today, my feet walk me into Mildred's room. MILDRED HANSEN, the sign on the door reads. I step in and am rocked back. The woman who's lying on the bed is hooked up to all sorts of hissing, whirring, beeping machines. Her large grey eyes are wide open in a frozen look. Her chalky-white skin and rigid limbs signal a serious condition.

Stroke, my mind tells me.

God, what would you have me do here?

I pull a chair close to her bed, sit down, lean in and whisper, 'Mildred ...'

There's a brief flicker, a slight widening of the ocean eyes.

'Can you hear me?'

Another flicker.

I know she hears me. Immediately, I know what I must do. I reach inside my bag, pull out a well-worn copy of Margaret Fishback Powers' *Footprints in the Sand* and turn the pages. In the secret space of my heart that I trust, I know exactly what I am meant to do.

The sound of my voice and the words on the page build a bridge between us. The machines continue to hiss and whir. Mildred continues to stare. I continue to read, the sound of my voice filling the space, substituting for hugs, feelings and reassurances.

With each encounter, the words of my masters are beginning to shine as truths in my heart.

There is nothing to do. I only need to be.

47

'ALL I DO IS GIVE MY MONEY AWAY. BILLS, BILLS, BILLS ...'
A long, weary sigh. An armchair sags under Girish's deepening
despair. A cold sweating bottle of Sam Adams waits, his lone
companion.

Ohmygodohmygodohmygod

Amma's singsong chant, the spiritual soundtrack of my
childhood 'Shuklaambaradharam Vishnum Shashivarnam
Chathurbhujam ...'

If there's a God, where is He in all this? How convenient to
be invisible, formless, in everything and nothing, now here and
nowhere.

'When I chased money, I never had enough. When I got my
life on purpose and focused on giving of myself and everything
that arrived into my life, then I was prosperous.' – Dr Wayne Dyer

Ohmygodohmygodohmygod

'You volunteer full-time!? But that's something old, retired
people do. You're so young. Or may be very rich,' she cackles,
delighted by her humour.

Dear Parent,
Given the rising costs of an education that is designed not
just to teach, but prepare your sons and daughters to take on the
world, the college will be raising the cost of tuition ...

Feel your heart space. Ask what really matters. All your soul desires is expansion.

Nicor	$100.00
AT&T	$85.00
Meijer	$78.26
Honda	$230.00
Mortgage	$1,045.00

Know who you really are. Be who you came here to be.

'... must I fear what others fear?
Should I fear desolation when there is abundance?
... other people strive for fame
I avoid the limelight.
... I drift like a wave on the ocean
I blow as aimless as the wind.
... all men settle in down their grooves
I alone am stubborn and remain outside.'

– 20th verse of the Tao Te Ching

Dear Diary,
It's such a struggle, this moral dilemma. The voice in my heart roars: serve, serve, serve. And yet, I live in a dollars-and-cents world. Sometimes, nothing makes sense. Am I stupid? Or do I continue to be guided by The Great Truth that I Am ...?

Breathe In.
Breathe Out.
Connect with the Highest Truth of Who You Are.

'Discover why some of the richest people in the world are not millionaires. They are volunteers.' – Erma Bombeck

I owe, I owe, so off to work I go ...

'You have been taught to live in fear. You have been told about the survival of the fittest and the victory of the strongest and the success of the cleverest. Precious little is said about the glory of the most loving. And so you strive to be the fittest, the strongest, the cleverest – in one way or another – and if you see yourself as something less than this in any situation, you fear loss, for you have been told that to be less is to lose.' – 'God' in *Conversations with God* by Neale Donald Walsch

48

'Would you stop by Cheryl today?' Daisy, the floor manager at the nursing home, asks.

'Sure,' I reply.

Daisy points me in the direction of Cheryl's room and starts to describe her case, but is interrupted by an assistant with a problem: a screaming resident who insists someone killed her baby.

'I'll look in on her,' I say, as Daisy looks first at me, then her assistant confused about who to attend to.

Cheryl is in 139. Her skin is pale, the trace of spidery blue veins just beneath the surface. She shares a room with three others and occupies the middle bed. Her baby-blue gown has ridden halfway up her thighs, her legs are splayed. I adjust the gown so her adult diaper isn't exposed for the entire world to see. I lean down and look into her eyes: vacant, expressionless pools of grey-green.

'Cheryl …' I whisper, not wanting to startle her.

She turns towards me, eyes roaming my face. I have no idea what she sees, if she registers anything.

Cheryl is a stroke victim.

She's too young to be trapped inside her body.

She reaches out a hand, as if groping in the dark, searching for a hand-hold. I offer my hand. Her skin is cool, baby-soft. She holds tight, like a child threatened by the boogeyman.

I sit beside her and start to talk. 'I'm here. I'm not going anywhere.'

I stroke her forehead with my other hand. 'God loves you, honey. I know it's difficult for you to believe that, but He does care. Who knows why stuff happens? Somehow we let God take the rap. I'm guilty of that too, believe me. But I know now in a way I've never known before that God does care.'

Cheryl keeps her head cocked to the side, listens. Her eyes are calm, focused, like she's absorbing a nugget of wisdom.

I wonder if she understands what I'm saying.

It doesn't matter. It truly does not. There's a part of me that knows the spirit inside can sense, hear the emotion in the voice, connect with the energy one brings into the space. That's what I focus on, showing up as all of who I am.

After all, we're both energy beings. The vibrations take over, when all else fails.

When I look at her again, I notice a tear run down the side of her face.

She's feeling something.

I rub her hand, continue to speak to her.

Soon, Cheryl is crying, soft hiccupping sobs. I shush her, smooth the wispy brown hair from her slightly damp forehead. I think of what her story might be. This woman, now reduced to a body with a feeble mind, once had a job to go to, a home to run, and children to raise. She cooked and shopped and chauffeured her kids to band practice and ballet classes. May be her husband is trying to hold it all together now. May be there is no husband. May be she is a single woman. Or a single mom with a different story.

One thing I do know. *She's lonely, lost and afraid.*

———⋘≫⋙———

My meditation practice keeps me centred and grounded. Some mornings I do a guided meditation, others I use meditation CDs, and some days I just sit and breathe and chant.

Most times I like to begin my day with a piece of spiritual literature. My staples are Dr Wayne Dyer, Eckhart Tolle, and

Thich Nhat Hanh. My union with God feels stronger. I feel guided, inspired, connected.

My weekly group at The Palms is going strong. Other weekdays, I volunteer at the community and a nursing home, I write, I learn, I read. My life has a pace, a routine, a rhythm. It is not a pace the world understands or appreciates, but that has little relevance to me now.

50

HOSPICE.

The word pops up in conversations at the retirement community, always whispered in sombre tones with serious facial expressions. It appears in books I'm reading. It shows up at the library in a flyer propped up on the display desk. It's that word again.

Hospice.

I'm not even sure what it means. A service in a hospital, perhaps. May be it is a specific hospital department. An aspect of a hospital wing? I've never, ever heard the word before, not before I moved to the US.

I have learnt well. When a sign keeps showing up , I am meant to pay attention. Something popping up time and again is not some random coincidence. At first, it's a soft whisper. Then it becomes a faint nudge. And, if you still don't pay attention, it develops into a persistent niggle.

There are no accidents or coincidences, I know, in a perfect universe. I am meant to pause, take notice and listen for guidance.

Except, what am I meant to do with a word I don't even know the meaning of? For one thing, I could simply ask someone just like I did when I encountered the word 'popsicle'. Or I could pull out a dictionary and look up the word.

I do neither. Life traps me in its net and I get caught up preparing my Monday group questionnaire, or chauffeuring Ruki to play rehearsals, or busy 'saving the world', as Girish would say. Somehow, the little detail of the word and what it means slips through the cracks.

Friday afternoon. My cell phone rings. It's my friend, Chris.

'Hey! What're you doing this evening?' he wants to know.

'Ummm … nothing, really. Girish is overseas on business. It's just Ruki and I. We'll probably watch a chick flick or something.'

'Wanna go watch a play?'

'Sure. Ruki would love that too.' A committed theatre buff, Ruki's always game to watch drama unfold on a stage.

'Great,' he says. 'It's a staged reading in Elgin. We could pick you up at half-past six.'

'Perfect.'

As soon as I hang up, I have an uh-oh moment. I forgot to ask what play we're going to. Never mind. Knowing Chris's tastes in theatre, it's got to be good.

———————— ◦•◦ ◦•◦ ————————

The sweet-fragrance of perfumes mingles in the air as we slip into our seats. Men and women shrug off heavy jackets. Pink-cheeked winter faces abound around us. There's a low murmur of greetings and conversations as friends and family shuffle towards their seats.

Soon, a gentleman steps up on stage and launches into the housekeeping rules before giving the audience a brief background of the staged reading. The play is titled *Confessions of a Reluctant Caregiver*.

Since it is a staged reading, the props are in place on stage and the actors take their positions, scripts in hand. The audience settles down, anticipation peaking.

Within ten minutes, I am absorbed in the plot and the characters. It hits close, the theme of a daughter caring for her mother who is dying of cancer as the father struggles with the looming reality of a lonely existence. The characters' conversations around death are awkward, stilted.

It is such a well-scripted play that time goes by so fast and the reading is over before I know it. A well-dressed woman takes stage and announces that she is from a hospice.

There it is again, that word.

I've ignored the whispers and nudges and niggles. This time, the Universe had to hurl a brick to the middle of my forehead to get my attention. It's impossible to ignore, the theme of the play and the hospice connection.

I get it, God. You've got my attention. Now please tell me what I'm meant to do with it.

The lady from hospice makes a short presentation. As soon as she opens the floor for questions, my hand shoots up.

'Are you looking for volunteers?' I ask.

'Volunteers are the backbone of our organization. We couldn't do without them,' she responds. 'If you're interested and would like more information, we have flyers on display in the back of the room. Our website is on the flyers. If you have any further questions, I'd be happy to answer them.'

She smiles at me.

I need no further invitation. I grab a handful of literature on our way out. On the drive home, Chris asks if I'm serious about volunteering at hospice.

'Well, I wasn't even sure what the word meant until this reading,' I say. 'And the lady from hospice explained it well. Strange thing is, this sign keeps coming at me. I know I'm meant to do something with it.'

'So, does it sound like something you'd like to be involved in?' Chris knows the back story of my parents' loss eighteen months apart.

'I'm going to check their website. That's the next step. I know enough to pay attention when a sign keeps knocking on my door,' I say, wondering what this is leading to.

As I pore over the hospice website the next day, I find myself wishing we'd had hospice care for Amma and Appa back home in India. In saying 'no more' to chemotherapy and opting for pain management, that is pretty much what we achieved for Amma. She died at home in her bed. Appa passed on at the hospital with all four of his children caring for him in his last days.

When I click on the 'Volunteer' link, I see a volunteer training programme scheduled for two weeks from now. I do the only thing I can: I sign up.

It all seems to be lining up, ducks in a row. This is no random coincidence. This is precise cosmic channelling.

———————<‹ ›‹ ›>———————

When Girish and I got engaged, I'd given him a tiny card with the words: Let's walk hand in hand even when we don't see eye to eye. Little did I know then that it would become the theme of this phase of our married life.

My husband doesn't always understand the roads I navigate. But I feel him holding my hand all the way. Raised to embrace the values of hard work and commitment, he soldiers on in the battlefield of the corporate world – letting me nurture my dreams and follow my passions. It's a lot more than I can ask for. I am blessed.

And God, my CEO, continues to provide for all our needs. We continue to be grateful for our lives every single day.

A marriage is organic. Each of us is constantly changed, grown, and forced to evaluate our priorities. That our tree of togetherness is firmly rooted in love is what sustains us on life's journey.

We love each other.

We're committed to each other.

And a love like that isn't an ordinary thing.

51

*I*T IS THE MORNING OF THE TRAINING PROGRAMME. I HAVE the ominous feeling that I'm about to visit the House of Death today. When I step inside the double doors, however, the interiors have none of the menacing mystery of death. The feeling is warm, homely with earthy colours and a welcoming group of people.

There are about fifteen volunteers. All day long we talk about death and dying, end-of-life issues, the families' anger at God. I learn that this is where people on the last legs of their earthly journey die in peace. There is even an opportunity to rebuild broken relationships and mend fences. How can such a place be anything but an oasis of serenity and spirit?

It occurs to me then what a remarkable opportunity this would be to make a difference in the life of someone who is, perhaps, at the loneliest stage of life. Death is at the door and there is fear of what lies beyond the door. If I can touch someone, offer a listening presence to the stories of their life – all the parts, the good, bad and ugly – I could facilitate a peaceful transition.

Right after the training programme, I am so energized and enthused about the vision and mission of this organization that I'm ready to rename the space 'The House Of Hope'.

As I wait in the foyer for my husband to pick me up, an ambulance drives up to discharge a patient. The man on the gurney looks pale. A few minutes later, the paramedics wheel in an old woman hooked up to oxygen. I glance at them, wonder how much time they have, what their life stories are.

I feel like an insider. I know death. I've been in the same room as *it*. I've seen a parent I love reduced to an inanimate, lifeless and rigid body. I know that pain.

More importantly, I know I'm a piece in the rich, diverse tapestry of humanity. We're all connected, even without knowing each other. These patients, their families and I, we're meant to connect now, at this moment in space and time, in the final season of this person's life.

My heart tells me that God is calling me to do something here. The devastation of loss, the searing pain of grief I suffered, has led me to this precise moment, so I can reach deep inside and find healing while helping others find it too. All I have to do is show up with all the love and compassion in my heart.

Epilogue

JOHN'S BODY IS STILL WARM. HE HAS BEEN DEAD SINCE half an hour.

The drapes are drawn. The room is dark.

The family is off making funeral arrangements.

It is just John and I now.

He looks still, serene.

This is John's body, the empty shell; his soul is probably hovering over us in the thin air of the room.

I join my palms together, close my eyes and say a quiet prayer.

John and I did not know each other in life; but I do know him now. We have co-created this moment. It is a sacred moment, a moment there are no words for. I feel its sanctity in the centre of my being.

For I know now, that John is not dead. I know now that death is neither a beginning nor an end. That life is simply the beginning of a new form; that the act of dying is walking through the door to another life.

My heart is healed. My soul is well. I know that the journey that began with Amma's passing has been about finding my true North, my home.

In this moment, I know I have found home. I am home.